WELSH FOOD STORIES

Carwyn Graves

2022

www.uwp.co.uk

British Library Cataloguing-in-Publication Data
A catalogue record for this book is available from the British Library.

ISBN: 978-1-91527-900-2

Illustrations and cover artwork by Elise Tel
Typeset by Marie Doherty
Printed by CPI Antony Rowe, Melksham, United Kingdom

CONTENTS

I Miriam ac Arthur

*Yn y gobaith y byddwch yn gallu mwynhau cynnyrch toreithiog
y winllan hon mewn blynyddoedd i ddod, a'i rannu'n hael ...*

Ac i Dadcu a Valerie, Mamgu a Dado

*Chi oedd fy nolen i'r gorffennol, yn 'estyn
yr haul i'r plant, o'u plyg'.*

*I chi y mae'r diolch am y parch dwfn at y rhai a'n rhagflaenasant,
am y fraint o gael dysgu beth yw bwyd da, go iawn, ac
am eich ffydd yn yr Un a greodd y daioni hyn i gyd.*

FOREWORD

by Patrick Holden

Since arriving here on our windswept hillside in western Wales as a member of a 'back to the land' hippy commune in the 1970s, we have been playing our own tiny part in creating some modern Welsh food stories. Although our big food project is now Hafod, our raw milk cheese made on the farm from the milk from our herd of Ayrshire cows, before that we milled wheat and sold flour to local wholefood shops from wheat grown on the farm, and grew carrots and other vegetables, driving them up to London to supply Cranks, a pioneer vegetarian restaurant.

Wales is not currently famous for its food culture or as a supplier of high-quality traditional artisanal foods to distant markets, arguably due to the impact of the twentieth century food system industrialization which almost annihilated the last remnants of the traditions which used to exist throughout the country. But over the decades since arriving here, I've often wondered about the strivings of the food producers of Wales who preceded my brief occupancy of this hill, memories of whose food stories lie largely forgotten, buried in the landscape which has been a silent witness to everything that happened here, only fragments of which are perhaps still dimly recalled by the descendants of those land stewards, but many of which have been obscured by the cloak of history.

It was the Irish mystic, poet and bard John O'Donohue who described landscape as cultural memoria, holding out against transience and revealing to the sensitive the stories of what went before;

so what an absolute delight to read this book, which quite literally unearthed Wales's precious and fascinating food cultural history through the prism of half a dozen of its staple foods.

How wonderful to learn, for instance, that at Felin Ganol, Andrew and Anne Parry have managed to reinstate the tradition of producing flour from a wheat variety which is specifically adapted to the unique terroir of the Welsh soils and climate. For me, this was all the more exciting, given my involvement with an initiative led by my great friend Peter Segger in 1975, the aim of which was to reinstate the mill to produce real flour, which never got off the ground. As a cheddar producer, it was also inspiring to learn that Wales has at least some justification to claim its place in the history of UK cheddar production. Perhaps the most heartening element of the book is its focus on current producers who in different ways are striving to reinstate Wales's forgotten food cultural heritage. As Carwyn remarks at the end of the book, this renaissance has come in the nick of time, at the very moment when some of the language used to describe unique elements of Welsh food culture is only now remembered by those over seventy.

Lesser mortals might spend a lifetime of haphazard research and discover only a few food history fragments, so how lucky we are and how indebted we should feel to Carwyn Graves, who has performed a great service in uncovering the food stories which constitute such a key element of the rich cultural history of Wales, and within it so many components of what we need for a relocalized food system with a future. Carwyn is deserving of our gratitude and respect. His assiduous exploration of the history of the food culture of Wales makes fascinating reading.

Patrick Holden
Bwlchwernen Fawr, Ceredigion

INTRODUCTION

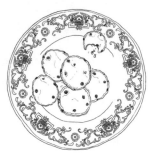

On Welsh food stories ...

I am standing on a gusty, tussocky hilltop in mid-August. Streaks of sunlight reach me as the clouds, only a few dozen metres above my head, billow past. Every now and then, a few drops of light rain wet my cheeks. Behind, where the heather-brown hills rise yet higher, the clouds have run into each other and shed curtains of rain across the landscape. But before me and below me lies a green vale bathed in sunlight – here, out of the wind, a patchwork of small fields, ancient woodlands and hedgerows shelter solid, old farmhouses and fields of corn. And beyond this, the coastal lowland, beaches of holidaymakers and then the sea, shimmering in the sun. This is a familiar landscape to me – but it's also an ancient, neglected foodscape.

This same scene – from the Glamorgan ridgeway near Cardiff – could have been located in almost any part of my home country of Wales. On the Clwydian range of the north-east borderlands near Liverpool. Near Harlech, in the north-west facing out to Ireland. In the Preseli hills of the old south-western kingdom of Dyfed. Or where it did, on the Glamorgan hills of the sheltered south-east. For

WELSH FOOD STORIES

unlike northern France, central England or northern Germany, all
parts of northern Europe otherwise broadly comparable to Wales
in latitude and climate, Wales is a world of microcosms.

Welsh food has reflected the country's kaleidoscopic landforms
and has traditionally been marked by great variation. There were
significant differences between the diets on the coasts and the river
valleys, where grain could be grown and most of the towns and all
the ports were located, and the mountainous interior, with worse
growing conditions and climate and so more dependence on hardy
animals. The country, one of the cradles of the modern science of
geology, is underlain by a startling range of bedrock types. These
matter for food; dramatic limestone outcrops rise on parts of both
north and south coasts, and provide rich, alkaline soils good for a
range of crops.

Only a few miles inland from the limestone belt in the north,
much of mountainous Snowdonia is composed of ancient igneous
rock, the product of volcanic activity 500 million years ago. This
slow-weathering rock is why these venerable mountains are still
standing, despite millennia of grinding down by ice, wind and rain.[1]
Infertile and cold, here the fields can contain more stone than soil.
This harsh terrain led to specific ways of living, farming and eating
that in some ways had more in common with the inhabitants of the
Alps a thousand miles away than with lowland neighbours only a
few miles downhill. In other parts, layers of sandstone gave rise to
rich broad valleys of deep red soil to gladden farmers' hearts. And
then there are the mudstone and siltstone moorlands that cover
such a broad swathe of the middle of the country, the fertile lias
lowlands of Glamorgan and the large coastal expanses of shifting
saltmarsh and duneland, home to diverse ecosystems and some of
the world's best lamb.

Geography and geology set the parameters of the possible for ways of farming and living, but people are never fully captive to their circumstance, and can organize themselves to overcome some of the constraints put upon them by their surroundings – often in search of good food. This is true of course of any society, from the pastoralist Tuareg people of Niger to the fishing cultures of south-east Asia. In Wales when the ice receded after the end of the last ice age, people followed – or preceded – the trees and vascular plants that recolonized this stretch of what was at the time the north European continent.[2] They found a land that combined three of the most basic elements needed for good food: earth, in all the rich variety of Welsh soilscapes; sea, with the bounty of the shore and deeper waters; and fire, with the fuel provided by coal and peat against the nagging winter cold and the wet. Some of the foods this new land produced and sustained continued to be cultivated or harvested through the rest of recorded history, as we shall see. It's possible to make too much of continuities of this sort, and yet there is something to be pondered in the discovery of large Iron Age middens of cockles on the shores of the Burry Inlet, in the same estuarine landscape that still sustains Wales's greatest cockle fishery to this day, or the survival of the pastoral tradition centred around cattle, sheep and goats that has such prominence in the oldest Welsh and Irish mythology and literature.

But Wales's food story is marked as much by dramatic change as by continuity. Geology and geography conspired to set the course of the country's food and farming in ways that amplify trends which the rest of the Western world experienced to a perhaps lesser degree. The particular range of bedrock types that underlie much of the country led to it being the first society in the world to be fully industrialized, according the UN's definition, with only a third of the labour force working on the land as early as 1851.[3] Copper in the Swansea area led to mines being sunk there as far back as the 16th century, and even in counties like Ceredigion, traditionally regarded as pastoral backwaters, lead mining had created an industrial El Dorado by the 1730s. The primary fuel for the country's early industrial boom lies in the rich veins of coal under what became known as the south Wales coalfield, where the bedrock was literally burnt up to fire the furnaces of the largest steel and copper works the world had ever seen. Before that, it had already provided plentiful employment for centuries, cheap fuel for burgeoning towns, bread ovens and salthouses on the nearby coast. All this had a significant effect on food and farming, as Welsh society's conception of itself shifted well before most other societies from that of an agrarian/pastoral worldview to one shaped by the forces of industry and early capitalism. That this happened in a society that had already been moulded for centuries by early colonialism[4] means that the history of Welsh food displays in a more extreme form some of the forces that have shaped food worldwide for the past two hundred years.

Food history?

Throughout Welsh history, and starting well before the English conquest, much of the best bounty of the land was reserved to particular groups or classes. These differences between social classes were often marked, during some periods even more than others. As we emerge into post-Roman recorded history, we find that the landless peasant classes, particularly during times of crisis and famine, often suffered badly and their diet during these periods was pitiful. But Welsh society at all times also contained free farmers and smallholders, as well as wealthy and well-connected landowners, who

4

had a more stable economic basis and had access to much more variety in food. Looking at the last thousand years in search of the stories of Welsh food, that simple, evocative phrase, 'Welsh food' is much more problematic than it sounds. Whose Welsh food – and where and when?

The historiography and study of Welsh food, such as it is, has largely been dominated either by accounts of rural hardship, or of working-class Victorian poverty.[5] The pastoral economy of upland Wales has typically been regarded as providing the meanest of fare, with oats and dairy predominating, and simple dishes cooked on backward implements.[6] There is more than a little truth in this. During the 16th century, for instance, the abject poor were estimated at 30% of the population, and they typically dwelt in one-roomed hovels lacking windows and chimneys. The basic component of the lowest class's pre-20th century diet would have been oat gruel with dairy products or meat only featuring when available. Female members of this social class in Anglesey were so well known for their persistent begging for cheese, butter and milk that they were known as *gwragedd cawsa* (cheese gatherers).[7] But even for the lowest class, the trope of particular Welsh poverty does not hold; during the era of the workhouse and the working poor, for instance, the British food enquiry of 1863 noted that the Welsh labouring classes were better fed than their English counterparts.[8] Some of these people had the advantage of the sea within easy access; seaweed to fertilize fields and potato patches, oysters cheaper than eggs, and dependable herring salted from the brine.

A good proportion of the population from the sixteenth century onwards were small farmers and smallholders – usually around 50%. In favoured corn-growing areas such as the Vale of Glamorgan or Pembrokeshire, these could be relatively prosperous. The antiquarian and naturalist George Owen (1552–1613) noted that in his native Pembrokeshire 'the poorest husbandman liveth upon his own travail, having corn, butter, cheese, beef, mutton, poultry and the like of his own sufficient to maintain his house ...', and went on to note that even these poorer sorts were generally able to eat meat on a daily basis. Labourers ate less well by his calculation, but were not restricted to a subsistence diet in this pre-industrial era: their annual food consumption was 6.5 bushels of oats, one bushel of oat malt, ¾ Cardigan stone of cheese, 1.5 gallons of butter and half a quarter of meat. This was supplemented by what they could grow or buy of vegetables (leeks, cabbages, onions, peas, beans) together with eggs and scraps of meat.[9]

These semi-independent farmers, although subject to times of crisis and famine, generally had the resources to enjoy a varied diet, at least for most of the year. The bounty of the natural world – wild plants of all sorts, eggs and small game – all contributed to this. The earliest Welsh laws, attributed to the 10th century king, Hywel Dda, codify in great detail the value of different foodstuffs and illuminate how the varied bounty of the land was used in his era: honey, pigs, fruiting trees and sea-trout were all accorded particular values, and all featured in comfortable Welsh diets of the time and later eras. The 12th century historian, Gerald of Wales, notes how the typical Welsh diet of his day consisted primarily of meat and dairy, in contrast to the grain- and gruel-eating lowland dwellers of England and France, precisely due to the upland nature of much of the country.

Meat and dairy are of course nutrient-rich, and although the cheese-loving Welsh were sometimes sneered at by their neighbours to the east, this was far from starvation fare by any means. But beef and dairy, which many parts of Wales specialized in, could also bring riches to less well-endowed regions too by virtue of the access they gained to mercantile towns and cities in England. As early as the 1540s, two Anglesey drovers, Rhys ap Cynfrig and Rhys ap Llywelyn, had grown rich exporting cattle to markets in the English Midlands,[10] and over the ensuing two centuries the drovers' trade would create early banking systems and bring great wealth to middling farmers in Snowdonia. One of the consequences of this was that the beef that had become the cornerstone of the region's prosperity became itself unknown in people's diets – the cattle were now a commodity for the market.

Above these labouring and small farmer classes were the members of the professions, merchants and wealthier craftsmen and yeomen, who constituted around 15% of the population. These dwelt on established farmholdings across the countryside, or constituted an upwardly mobile urban class. Small towns across Wales are known to have remained reasonably prosperous at times of agrarian crisis in England, most likely due to their early specialization in animal products (such as wool and hides) and cattle markets.[11] Their stability created an urban market for luxury products, including food products. Goods stocked by a Llanfyllin mercer (a small town in the hills of Montgomeryshire) in 1670 included wares as varied as glazed cloth, silk fabric and fur, bodices, silver cuffs, gallons of ink, mirrors, satin capes for children as well as currants, sugar, spices, brown candy and tobacco.[12]

With easy access to an even greater range of items than this were the aristocratic class, whose fortunes also waxed and waned, but who throughout Welsh history enjoyed the best luxury foods of the period, be that imported wine, or Conwy-grown greenhouse figs.[13] Even during the centuries of war and upheaval of the Middle Ages, Welsh princes and nobles enjoyed sumptuous feasts, of which their poets sang paeans of praise which have survived to the present day. One such treatise, Peniarth 147, details the wide range of meats, fish, soups, vegetables, and sweets that were served in contemporary feasts. It mentions an array of breads, meat and fish; choice vegetables, 'exotic fruits like oranges and grapes, sugar and spices, and a bewildering array of imported wines to pour down thirsty throats, together with the native beer, cider, and metheglin' (the latter two beverages form an interesting case study in the effects of changing fashions and social mores on ways of eating and drinking, which we look at in chapter 7).[14]

These upper classes benefited from the generally peaceful conditions in Wales from the 14th century onwards, in marked contrast to both Ireland and many parts of the near continent – all of which impacted on agriculture, commerce and food. This allowed them to invest in landed estates, gardens, deer parks, melon houses and orangeries in a comparable way to their English peers at court, giving Welsh gardeners, butlers and housemaids glimpses and perhaps tastes of a broad range of foods outside their home experience.

Distinctive?

The Welsh food landscape was, then, a varied one which saw changes over time as economic fortunes waxed and waned. An important point that arises from this is that reducing traditional Welsh food, as many have done, to the food of the nineteenth century rural and working poor is to take a (usually urban, middle class) prejudice against certain foodstuffs and ways of life, and to flatten a food landscape that was massively varied – geographically and socially, as well as chronologically. Recent food historians, such as Joan Thirsk in the case of England or Erwin Seitz for Germany have emphasized in their approach to food history the use of contemporary accounts of what people ate and applied the basic principle that humans have a propensity to follow fashions. That peasants would work as gardeners or cooks in an aristocratic Great House, and not try to emulate what they saw when at work in their own gardens or kitchens, is an unlikely proposition – and no less so in Conwy than in Cologne. And to posit that the Welsh, almost uniquely, were so culturally conservative and resistant to change in their habits that this did not happen, is to ignore the overwhelming evidence of building styles, religious upheaval and clothing, not to mention the rapid and well-documented spread of food innovations such as the potato or tea-drinking within the country.[15] (We could also at this point mention the falling out of fashion of rye, and the disappearance of drinks like mead and *diod griafol*, to underline the obvious point that the tides of fashion in Wales as elsewhere both bring in the new and sweep away the old.)[16]

Traditional Welsh food is, then, in many senses a misnomer for a varied and ever-changing tapestry of practices, influences and raw ingredients that differed both through society and across the country. Partly, this is to do with Wales's varied cultures: parts of Wales in language, building style, farming practice and underlying geology feel much like lowland England or Normandy. Wander the lanes of south Pembrokeshire, Gower or Monmouthshire in high summer, and you'd be forgiven for thinking you were in Dorset or Somerset. But travel the coast road between Barmouth and Harlech, or venture down the Llŷn Peninsula or along the western coast of Anglesey, attentive to the vernacular architecture, place names, flora and climate, and you would conclude that Wales is in fact in its atmosphere much more akin to Gaelic Ireland or coastal Brittany. But this point can also be over-emphasized. There are distinctive threads in the whole fabric of Welsh food history that are particularly long-lasting, or particularly prominent in comparison to the diets of these neighbouring cultures and peoples – England, Ireland, northern France and Scotland – and we will follow some of these threads in the chapters to follow. And where these threads are combined with a culture – particularly Welsh-language culture – that has inhabited this swathe of earth since quite literally time immemorial, where every field, every stream, every outcrop has a name stretching back centuries or millennia, that is resistant to change and that views itself as indigenous in a number of important senses – you have the recipe for a food culture distinct in several interesting ways.

One of those is a fondness for leeks and cheese among the Welsh, which has been noted by outside observers and native commentators since the early Middle Ages. Similarly, the widespread use of shellfish and seaweed by the coastal population was often pointed out as distinctive. In 1775, for example, this description of the fare of the inhabitants of Anglesey by an outsider notes with surprise that: 'they eat little meat, but eat cheese and butter, bacon, tame and wild fowls, sea fish, oysters, crabs, lobsters, shrimps, prawns, mussels and cockles'.[17] Grain culture in Wales stands at the intersection of a 'Celtic' oat-based tradition and a northern European wheat/barley/rye tradition, producing a heritage both of griddle cakes (of which Welsh cakes have been the longest surviving example) and of loaves. The historic cider making regions of the world are surprisingly limited in number and area, and south-eastern Wales is of global importance in the development of this usually underappreciated tipple. And the pastoral tradition in Wales, though by no means unique, is also distinctive both in its longevity, stability and its comparative importance within society.

These threads coalesce for me in the recollections my grandfather, Dewi Lloyd Lewis, shared with us often, of his and his siblings' food growing up in the hills of Pembrokeshire in the 1930s.

Unable to speak fluent English until he did a correspondence course at the age of 16, he hardly travelled further than a 10-mile radius from home throughout his childhood on the family smallholding. Our family line in that part of the Carmarthenshire / Pembrokeshire borderlands extends back over 400 years and much of the food my grandfather ate will, in all likelihood, have been recognizable to his forebears centuries beforehand. Oats were a mainstay of the family diet, and he would have porridge for breakfast every day for the rest of his life. His brother fondly recalls trips to the coast in season to harvest cockles by hand using the old methods. Cakes in the usual sense of the word in English were not a part of the diet: rather, treats consisted of those baked goods that could be produced with a griddle: pancakes and Welsh cakes amongst them. Leeks were among the most important of the vegetables grown in the veg patch, and cawl and bread were much in evidence. Cheese was adored, and buttermilk one of the most common drinks of all. In all of these ways and more, their diet was characteristic of so many of the food traditions and practices that had grown up in this land.

Many of these traditions have counterparts across western Europe and beyond, of course – but the particular combinations and emphases are unique to Wales, and form the basis of a forgotten but resilient cuisine, which though battered and bruised, has survived in its outline, and in some particulars, to the present day. My aim in writing this book is to bring to a wider audience the stories of several of these threads – some of the most important Welsh foods, their culture and the ways they have been shaped and perhaps mis-shaped by their custodians and wider social trends – and to use these stories as backgrounds to the exciting things food producers across the country are doing with them today, and which represent the continuation of each of these food stories.

Artisan tradition?

Referring to 'food stories' would seem to imply a kind of food culture that Wales is not often regarded, from the outside at least, as having. Many modern European countries boast a food culture rooted in traditions of farming and small-scale, quality production that have continued to this day. From the wines of Burgundy to Swiss cheesemakers and German bakers, a craft and a particular way of preparing foods have been handed down from generation to generation, from master to apprentice. This did not happen on the whole in 20th century Wales (or to a lesser extent, other parts of the British Isles), and early and widespread industrialization seems to be a major part of the reason. It would be the work of a – to my knowledge yet-to-be-written – PhD to delve into this, but, in Wales at least, two factors seem to have made all the difference: first, the generally rural nature of many food traditions in the face of the urbanity wrought by industrialization, coupled with the fact that these traditions were largely seen as belonging in the woman's domain.

These were 'farmhouse' traditions, whose practitioners and custodians were usually women, in both the Welsh-speaking core of the country and the traditionally English-speaking parts. This meant that food production tended to operate at the level of the household economy, even when production was for the market. This tradition – informal, networked, multi-generational – was enough to create and develop strong local food cultures across rural Wales that sustained a great breadth of practices, recipes and other food traditions, even with next to nothing in the way of interest from the literate upper classes. An early 20th century recollection of a Glamorgan farmhouse kitchen, with its features, vocabulary and memories, illustrates this well:

We had a very big kitchen, with a table to seat twelve to fourteen at a time, it was flagged and sprinkled with sand. I used to fetch this in a horse and trap from Cwm Ivy burrows. One house near us had a trodden earth floor, sprinkled with sand. Beams of course with hooks, huge dresser, settles and cupboard bed to one side of the hearth. One the other side was the pentan (hob). It was a vast fireplace, and more light came into the room through that than by the windows! You could see the stars if you looked up inside. There was a large oak beam supporting the inner wall of the chimney, massive thing it was, and that was called the clevvy place. And above that was the charnel, where you kept hams and things, that was a box-like structure going up above the ceiling ... We used a big brick oven for baking bread, it was in a back kitchen. I don't know how she did it, but my mother always managed to bake it perfectly, never overdone. She'd cook dowset in it too. That was like what we'd call custard tart, only it was about four inches thick. In winter we'd have shickan (=*sucan*) for breakfast. A sort of thick porridge. I remember my grandmother used to spend nearly an hour making that, sprinkling oatmeal bit by bit into a pan of boiling water. We'd have a couple of basins of that on the table, with a basin of milk for us to dip in and help ourselves. Then on sheep-washing days, in June, she used to make cheese cakes – these were made from curd, with a pastry like a turnover. My word, the women worked very hard in those days![18]

But when the cheap food that arrived with 20th century prosperity started threatening the household's monopoly on food, there were no guilds or long-established companies in Wales with an incentive to marketize and commodify what had been produced in the home or on the farm, unlike in some continental countries. After all, those with the knowledge and perhaps the greatest incentive to develop market access for food products in Wales – women – were not able to do so at any scale. On top of this, Welsh culture as such (in contrast to what was perceived as English, and modern) lived an increasingly threatened existence. It was defined by its strongest adherents – in the teeth of the strong currents of Anglicization and homogenization – as encompassing music, literature, religion and, to an extent, the visual arts. When native linguistic, literary or religious traditions were threatened, a stalwart class of farmers, teachers and ministers of religion rallied to their defence. Food, however, perhaps precisely because it was generally considered the woman's domain, was ignored – to the extent that native and often remarkably resilient traditions were on the whole unsuccessful in adapting themselves to mid-20th century society and economic conditions.

And so Caerphilly cheese, cockles, faggots and much else remained foods sold at small family-run market stalls. Welsh industry's contribution to this fate also seems clear: there was significantly less incentive to try and make money from food in Wales compared to unindustrialized parts of Europe, when better money was readily available in mining, quarrying and industry in many parts of the country. It's notable that the greatest commodification of Welsh food happened – oysters, beef, and the dairy trade – in those areas and eras where industry was least prominent.

As a result, when the last generation of cheesemakers, cockle-pickers, bakers (all women) and cider makers died out, their traditions in many cases died with them. There are, of course, some dishes, commodified by supermarkets or too deeply ingrained on people's palates to be forgotten, that survived and formed the late twentieth-century version of 'Welsh food'. Some of these – cawl, Welsh cakes, Welsh rarebit, laverbread – have retained an important place in people's diets and in their conception of Welsh food, as we shall see. But on the whole, and not uniquely in the Western world, Welsh food culture became during the latter decades of the twentieth century a thing conspicuous by its absence. Aside from the tourist-pleasing tidbits of Welsh cakes and Bara Brith, delectable as they are, and the strangely-named Welsh rarebit, Welsh food as category for most people both inside and outside Wales has become something of a blank. Mass-produced *bara brith* full of emulsifiers and glucose-fructose syrup does not a stake to a national cuisine make. That absence was all the more lamentable given what had preceded it: rich indigenous traditions, multifaceted yet uniform, enriched by outside influences and shaped by economic tides but, still, astonishingly stable for many long centuries.

A snapshot of all this was thankfully captured in the nick of time, just as these older ways of cooking, farming and eating were fading. The oral historian, Minwel Tibbott, happened to be employed by the right institution at the right time. In 1969, she was employed by the Welsh folk museum at St Fagans, and quickly started oral interviews with the oldest generation of women across Wales, whose memories reached back to the last decade or two of the 19th century. These remembered – and, in some cases, still continued to practise – old dishes, terms and ways of cooking that had been widespread but which, to society in general, were not much more than a memory. The painstaking work which Tibbott carried out, together with later research by Bobby Freeman and others, is invaluable to our appreciation of the whole of Welsh food history and the continuation of many practices even into the late twentieth century, and complements wonderfully the scattered observations we have of native food and eating habits from observers from the Middle Ages until the early 20th century. I have drawn extensively on their work (see the bibliography at the end of the book), as well as on observations made particularly by 17th and 18th century English travellers to Wales, with their detailed notes and curious outsiders' perspectives, for the picture I have been able to paint of traditional Welsh food throughout this book.

And this food heritage never disappeared from sight entirely. As we shall see, some of these age-old traditions clung on despite all that was against them. And alongside this, a new generation of food radicals grew up or came to Wales from the late 20th century onwards who valued much that the traditional ways embodied. As a result, Wales has been quietly pioneering much of the new local, artisan food scene, and has long had a significantly higher percentage of its land farmed organically than any other part of the UK (5% as of 2020, compared to an average of 2.6% for the other UK nations).

Natural riches

And so, before we tuck in to this nine-course meal of a book, let me presume to introduce Wales – this surprisingly diverse, rocky, sea-bound peninsula in north-western Europe – a second time. Green mountains sweep down to craggy coastlines. Cow-dotted fields and ancient moss-covered Atlantic oakwoods cling to the slopes. Limestone, sandstone and dark-bellied granite vie to outcrop. Fast-flowing streams tumble and trickle through the moss and the peat. Rivers race down the inclines, gathering tributaries and challenging salmon and sewin to keep jumping. Deep coastal rias open into rich, shallow waters. Regular rains water the ground, even as the tropical waters of the Gulf Stream keep the climate mild and temperate.

And people came. They named the nooks and the crannies, and ploughed a living from the land. They harnessed the watercourses with mills for flour. They tended orchards and vegetable gardens. They sang, they loved, they danced, they worshipped their God and they died. They hefted flocks to the hills, and shepherded them through rain, snow and sun. They fished the seas and they harvested the sands and the shallows. They made markets, and traded; they kept their foods and they changed them. They brought in what was new – tubers from the new world, sweet berries from the old – while still foraging, picking and gathering the leaves and drupes of their weather-worn realm. They feasted; they starved. They cursed the monotony; they praised the variety. Wales is a country whose landform shouts good food, and many of its inhabitants have been blessed to eat well for millennia. Let's take a bite into the stories of nine of those foods in turn.

Bwyta'n Te

Mae 'na rywbeth crefyddol yn y modd yr eisteddwn
Wrth y ford de, yn deulu cryno o dri.
Tydi, f'anwylyd, yn torri'r bara menyn, a hithau
Y fechan gochfochiog yn blaster o jam mwyar duon, a mi.
Ar wahân i'r dotio rhyfeddol
O gyfnewid byd gyda'n gilydd ... mae 'na de.

Fe gydnabyddai pawb
Fod y bwyd ynddo'i hunan yn fwynhau:
Cryfhau hefyd a wna'r ysbryd yn ei sgil.
Eto nid addoliad yw te ... Ond mae'n goresgyn
Pethau fel y bo'r ysbryd yn hopian yn hapus
Yn ein c'lonnau. Wrth inni dreulio carol nef
Yn ein cyfansoddiad 'rym yn gor, a'n gwddf
Yn cydblethu caloriau a geiriau gerbron
Yr Arweinydd anweledig a arlwyodd y ford.

Bobi Jones

1

BARA / BREAD

The texture of the loaf is nutty and slightly moist. It takes me back just a little to the dark breads I used to enjoy in Austria. But I am in Ceredigion, in the homely kitchen of Anne and Andrew Parry at Felin Ganol. Outside, spring is announcing its arrival in a thousand buds, and the stream – Wyre Fach – is coursing past the window. We'd come into the kitchen to talk, and Anne had offered me some *bara menyn* – bread and butter. 'Would you like to try some? It was baked four days ago, so it's a little stale ... but you're welcome to try it.'

As I bite into this particular loaf, I have good reason to pay full attention to the flavour. Lightly toasted, the crumb is immediately satisfying. I can tell this is bread that keeps its shape. It's dark, chewy, malty; more like rye bread than any normal wheat loaf. It has structure and depth. There are those deep notes some grains have. It's complemented wonderfully by the tangy, salty butter. It all tantalizes my tongue with a distinctive nutty wholeness that I turn around in my mouth for days after I've left Felin Ganol. The reason I am so interested in this slice of bread is that I am tasting the closest surviving thing to the breads eaten in Wales for centuries past. And I am eating it in the kitchen where the bread was baked, on the site where the flour was milled and only a few miles away from where the wheat is currently growing. All of these things are remarkable for a host of reasons.

Bara menyn

Bread – the essence of sustenance for millennia in Europe and much of the Old World – has roots that are as deep and as varied in Wales as any other native foodstuff. *Bara. Bara menyn. Bara brith. Bara planc. Bara can.* The profusion of bread-words in Welsh alone speaks volumes for the central place this foodstuff has in the country's cuisine, and consciousness. *Bara menyn* – bread and butter, or better, 'butterbread' – in particular evokes homeliness in a way almost nothing else can in Welsh. But scratch below the surface, and the astonishing thing about the story of Welsh bread is not so much its homely connotations, shared with cultures across northern Europe, as its sheer variety.

Variety in bread starts with geology. The underlying geology of different landforms leads to differing rates of erosion or protrusion – in this case, the hills and valleys of Wales. Higher altitude means buffeting winds and heavy rainfall. Soils become thin and acidic as minerals are leached downhill. The alluvial river valleys, already sheltered and drier, gain fertility. This patchwork of soils and soil quality dictates to a great extent what grains can be grown where. Rye in the coldest parts, where winters are long and summers all too short. Oats on the wet, westwards hills. Barley, wherever it would grow. Wheat on the best land of all, primarily the river valleys and sheltered lowlands of the east.

The poet David Thomas, writing in 1750, gives a first-hand depiction of each of Wales's 13 traditional counties according to their social customs. Food takes pride of place in his observations, and, if food is in question, then bread comes to the fore. His description furnishes us with a comprehensive snapshot of the grains – and thus breads – associated with different parts of the country in an era when local grains were the only ones available for local consumption:

Caernarfon (Caernarvonshire):

'*bara ceirch fydd yma lawer,*
o gaws, ymenyn a llaeth lawnder'
'Here is found oat-bread aplenty
and of cheese, butter and milk there's plenty'

Maesyfed (Radnorshire):

'*Bara rhyg yw'r ymborth amla*
Ymenyn caws sy'n aml ynddi'
'Rye bread is the people's sustenance
Cheese and butter are not uncommon'

Brycheiniog (Breconshire):

'*Haidd a gwenith, part o rygau*
Caws a 'menyn sydd mewn mannau'
'Barley, wheat – some ryebread too
Cheese and butter in parts they knew'

Mynwy (Monmouthshire):

'*Dyma'r fro gyfoethoca yng Nghymru*
Gwenith lawer iawn sydd ynddi ...
Pob yd ond rhyg sy'n hon yn tyfu
a'r bara gwenith goreu yng Nghymru'

'Here's the richest part of Wales
Wheat abounding in its vales
All grains but rye from here do hail
And the best wheatbread in all Wales'

How long this variegated map of grain growing had held sway in Wales by the time the poem was written is hard to know for certain, but the pattern of associating different grains with different parts of the country extends back into the mythological era of the Mabinogi and the triads. In the third branch of the Mabinogi, the greatest cycle of Welsh myths, one of the heroes, Manawydan, is thwarted by mice in his effort to grow wheat in what is modern-day Pembrokeshire. Similarly, 'Trioedd Ynys Prydein', or the Triads of the Island of Britain, are poetic groupings of symbolically significant places, people and objects, many of which were collected in the White Book of Rhydderch in the 13th and 14th centuries. One of them tells of Henwen, the sow, who 'in the Field of Wheat in Gwent gave birth to an ear of wheat and a bee, and since then the best wheat is to be found in that place. And from there she went on to Llonwen [perhaps Lannion] in Pembrokeshire, and there she gave birth to an ear of barley and a bee, and since that time the best barley is in Llonwen ...'.

This is confirmed by archaeological evidence suggesting that oats and barley were the principal crops in western parts of Wales, with wheat supplementing this and predominating in eastern parts, while rye was present at higher altitudes.[1] The volume of bread eaten by all strata of society is indicated by surviving records of the amounts kept in the storehouses of medieval castles under siege. Neath castle kept an entire garrison of soldiers fed for 58 days in 1316, with, amongst other things, 120 bushels of grain (what grain this was remains a tantalizing mystery) and 32 bushels of oat flour.[2] This is in stark contrast to Ireland, where there is a consensus that, away from the Normanized south and east, bread was not always widespread. The King's Council in Ireland comments in 1533, for instance, that the 'Irishry can live hardily without bread or other good victuals'. Such a statement could never have been made of the Welsh and their beloved *bara menyn*.

Of all these, wheat bread was widely regarded as the best of all. The medieval poets of the princes and nobility often specify that their patrons served only white wheat bread at their feasts – implying both that it was a status item and that it was therefore comparatively uncommon. The renowned bard, Iolo Goch, sings in praise of Owain Glyndŵr's court at Sycharth, in the north-east of the country, noting the presence of 'gwirodau, bragodau brig / pob llyn, bara gwyn a gwin' – 'spirits and finest braggot / every relish, white bread and wine'. More revealingly, an earlier court poet by the name of Iorwerth ap Cyriog (fl. *c*.1325–75) talks disparagingly of a diet consisting of 'bara o'r haidd a berw'r rhi / a dwfwr fu ymborth difri' – 'barley bread and watercress / and water was a sober diet',[3] implying that this was poor people's fare. This high regard for wheat's potential compared to other grains seems to have survived down the centuries: a particular favourite in centuries past seems to have been *myncorn* or 'maslin' bread, where wheat and rye were mixed, and which was considered in Wales to make a better bread than either grain by itself.

Not only was Welsh bread characterized by diversity in grains, but also by a genuine variety of baking methods, some of which were truly ancient. One of the specificities of Welsh bread baking was the common practice of doing so on a bakestone or griddle (cognate with the Welsh *gradell*), shared with the cultures of neighbouring Celtic countries. Griddles are referenced in the 10th century laws of Hywel Dda, and often turn up in inventories of Welsh landed gentry, yeomen and small farmers alike.[4] There was an entire culture that revolved around the bakestone, including specific iron tripods that would support the griddle over the fire, opinions as to which fuel was best for which types of baking, and a particular type of wooden spade or slice used for turning the loaves or cakes on the bakestone, the design of which varied from area to area. *Bara planc* was the one of the many names given to wheaten bread that was baked on griddles, and, as Freeman points out, maintaining a sufficient and even heat to bake bread on a bakestone using traditional fuels – gorse, peat, wood – required considerable skill.[5]

Breads of all sorts were made on the bakestone – barley loaves, unleavened loaves similar to the Irish soda bread, maslin bread and flavoured loaves such as gingerbread or caraway bread. Another widely used method was baking bread in a pot oven – a pot over a fire, covered with a lid in which bread was baked. Wall ovens tended to be known only in the larger, wealthier farmhouses, but the presence of bakestones in the inventories of gentry houses tell us that in many cases bakestone baking and the associated recipes were kept on even in those households that owned a wall oven. But in those cases, entire traditions built up in Wales, as in other northern European countries, of how the remaining heat should be used for other dishes and baked goods when the day's bread baking was done, sometimes shared with neighbours. By the early 20th century, with baking happening on a Saturday, this would often be Sunday's rice pudding.[6]

The most common grain over swathes of upland Wales was the oat, and a range of oaten breads were made. A note on translation is needed here: in Welsh, these are universally called *bara ceirch*, literally 'oat bread'. In English however, these would be known as oat*cakes* of various sorts. *Bara surgeirch* is one example: a sour oatmeal bread made by mixing oatmeal with wholemeal flour and slowly adding buttermilk to make a soft batter. This was poured onto a greased bakestone, and the mixture baked slowly on both sides over a moderate fire. *Bara ceirch* itself, often the staff of life and combined with other foods (such as fried cockles and eggs – see chapter 3), was made with little more than oatmeal, water, salt and dripping. The exact method varied from region to region, and often from family to family, but as anyone who has tried to make it at home knows, forming wafer-thin rounds as large as a dinner plate with fine even edges is no mean feat. Mastering the art of making a large quantity of perfect oatcakes was long considered one of the essential accomplishments for young women.

The diversity of grains in use here was supported by a dense web of mills for flour which sprang up in the Middle Ages. The Domesday Book records 6,000 mills in England as early as 1086, and records from church and abbey lands in Wales from this period confirm that they also existed in all corners of this country. As the population grew, so did the need for mills – not just for milling corn, but also for fulling and, later, for wool. The hilly nature of much of the country makes Wales prime watermill country, and gives the streams enough flow to make manipulation through mills worthwhile. This drew comment from early travellers to Wales, such as Samuel Johnson, who was amazed to find in 1774 eighteen mills in two miles of stream near Flint.[7] Cardiganshire alone by the 1850s had 150 corn mills, each one serving a dozen or couple of dozen households.[8]

But most of this rich tapestry of grains, breads and baking methods, and the organic mesh of grain-growing farmers, mills and bakers that upheld it, disappeared in the second half of the twentieth century. Just a few bakeries in the west of the country continued to produce *torth geirch* – oaten loaves, giving people a slender link to the past. But the mass production process known as 'Chorleywood', responsible for modern supermarket bread, was adopted wholesale by the surviving commercial bakeries. But the tradition of home baking, which had been a part of Welsh rural life for millennia, had roots enough to just about grow into the present day revival.

Felin Ganol

Felin Ganol – 'middle mill' – is the home of Andrew and Anne Parry, nestling in a fold of the hills near the sea in the old village of Llanrhystud, Ceredigion. The beautiful, stone-built, limewashed cluster of buildings is today one of only three traditional working watermills in Wales producing stoneground flour from grain – the other two being Y Felin in St Dogmaels and Talgarth Mill. Originally bought just to be a family home for the couple, their children and elderly parents, it has become today one of the hubs of the Welsh grain revival.

A cereal researcher by profession, there is beautiful poetic justice in the fact that Anne is now a miller, supplying stoneground, organic flour to local bakeries from locally grown grain, using a traditional, water-powered mill. When she and her husband, Andrew (responsible primarily for all the technical work needed to keep the mill going), arrived at Felin Ganol, they found the mill standing empty and idle next to the farmhouse, and initially had no intention of becoming millers. But though they hardly knew what everything was, they discovered that the old mill building was still full of milling equipment. 'It looked as if the last miller had just walked out,' Anne recounts, 'leaving even the hobnail boots on the mill floor ready to be used the next time.'

They decided to see whether they could get the mill to work. They flooded the old leat and mill pond – which they had mistaken for a strange, sunken lawn when they first viewed the house – and, with the help of many friends, managed to get the mill-wheel back on its bearing. It became evident quite quickly not only that the equipment could be made to work, but that something more could become of the project. Enquiries among neighbours and in the village brought to light a long and fascinating back-story to the mill, which had been in the same family – the Lewisiaid – for generations.

The original name of the mill, it turned out, was 'Moelifor' – now the name of a nearby farm. It had been a tithe mill, belonging to Moelifor house, an old estate going back to medieval times whose main building from the 1500s now lies under the roots of oak woodlands further up the valley. The location was perfect for a mill; on the cusp of the coastal plain next to the small Wyre Fawr river, a stone's throw from the spot where the old Aberystwyth road fords the river. It's difficult to imagine that the current mill building didn't have predecessors in the same spot in medieval times or even before; parish records for the current building suggest it was already standing in 1680. The farmhouse was of the old Welsh *croglofft* type, much extended over the generations. The mill building itself was extended with the increasing prosperity of the 18th and 19th centuries, leading to the characterful hodgepodge that stands there today.

The first named inhabitant of the house and mill was a certain John Thomas, who was paying tithes from this house in 1738. Through marriage and intermarriage, the tenancy of the mill and smallholding seems – intriguingly – to have passed down the female line of the same extended family for over two centuries. And, like many old families in western parts of Wales, they were a literary family who were key players in the local poetic scene. Thanks to this, their papers were given to the National Library of Wales in Aberystwyth in 1929. One of the men who married into the family was another poet, 'Eos Glanwyre' (1836–92), who was known locally for the large library he kept in the house. His entry in the Dictionary of Welsh Biography states that his compositions included *pryddestau*, lyrics and *englynion* (different metres of highly intricate Welsh poetry), many of which took prizes at eisteddfodau. The family was involved in the Baptist cause locally, with the mill-pond used for baptisms at times. Although they were sometimes seen to think of themselves as a cut above the rest, they were well regarded in the village.

They invested in the mill. There was an Anglesey stone on site, and in the middle of the eighteenth century a new French burrstone, made from stone quarried outside Paris, was installed alongside it. This gave a finer flour than the Anglesey grit, and shows the emphasis that local people put on quality – even if it came at the high price of £100, the equivalent of roughly £11,000 today. The old, native stone was kept to mill animal feed. In the 1850s, they built a kiln next to the mill to dry oats and wet grain, in order to improve the milling process during the all too frequent wet harvest seasons of western Wales.

By the turn of the 20th century, we have sufficient records to build a picture of a bustling and productive holding. In the adjoining garden and land was a kitchen garden, an orchard of apples, plums and walnuts, currant and gooseberry bushes, chickens and ducks. They kept cows, and made butter in the dairy next to the farmhouse kitchen. While goods such as sugar, tea and other treats would have been bought in, the mill represented a level of household resilience currently vanishingly uncommon in the Western world.

This resilience reflected the norm in their community, of course; the 1915 day book of milling records shows us what the people of Llanrhystud and the surrounding farms brought in to be milled: wheat, barley and oats, but also, latterly, rice and maize. The oldest generation in the village still remember bringing their grain in to be milled at Felin Ganol, before taking the flour home for their mothers to bake. At the height of operation, the mill was able to produce two tonnes of flour a week, from two millstones. Apart from rest days on Sundays, and work on the machinery in summer, when the water levels were lower anyway, the mill could produce that volume of flour year-round. This was intensive and highly-skilled work, with each type of grain requiring a different process: the husks of oats, for instance, stick to the oats and don't separate like wheat, so oats needed to be dried in the kiln before they could be milled.

The social changes that swept in after the Second World War changed the rural economy in Wales from top to bottom – albeit a little more slowly than in some other parts of western Europe. Government agricultural policy also played its part in encouraging a move away from mixed farming – short sightedly, perhaps. Grain growing tapered off in Ceredigion in the 1950s, and with it one of the main uses of the mill. The last members of the old family to live at Felin Ganol were siblings, Lewis, Elen and Dic Lewis. Dic, a real character, known locally as 'Dic y te' – 'Dick the tea' – ran a tea business from the barn. They employed another village man as miller, Dan Jones, who started working for the family at the age of 12 just before the First World War and whose wages in later years were £1 a week and a pound of butter. He last worked the mill at some point in 1958. The family sold the house after Elen's death in the 1970s, and the mill lay idle – but remained just as they had left it, right down to Dic's tea boxes.

The first grain that the Parrys bought to give the mill a test run was standard milling wheat. They opened the sluice gate, the mill wheel groaned and slowly started turning and, as they poured in the grain, the dead weight of the old French stones ground the wheat into flour. They were animated by a question that had been playing on Anne's mind for years: was the flour that people produced and used in mills like this in the past really the bland, gritty substandard stuff we are often led to believe it was? Seeing the waterwheel turning the second time I visit, on a blue March day, was a revelation. There are few images of food production and the agricultural cycle more deeply embedded within Western consciousness still today than that of the mill-wheel turning as the sluice gate is opened, water rushes down the millrace and onto the overshot wheel. The buckets on the wheel slowly fill, and with an imperceptible groan, the sheer weight of the water, ineluctably drawn downwards by gravity, pushes the wheel into motion. And behind and beyond the wheel itself, the wheel shaft, the crown wheel, and countless cogs shift into action and start turning the enormous millstones themselves. There are centuries of innovation, iterative learning and ultimately sophistication in the working of a traditional water mill or windmill, and seeing one in action on this Ceredigion stream is evocative of all sorts of things. There is a breathtaking beauty in realizing as you watch the wheel merrily turning that nothing more than the flow of water is capable of churning out kilos and kilos of flour; and with a little maintenance, nothing but a lack of water could cause the mill to run out of power or become otherwise incapable of its feat. The elegance of the solution is in its own way, humbling.

Unsurprisingly, perhaps, the mill's flour turned out to be good. So far, so good. But Anne knew that this milling wheat, from a modern cultivar grown in favourable wheat growing conditions, could not be the same as what the mill had ground originally. So, ten years ago, she and Andrew started asking around in the area to find where they could get their hands on locally grown grain. 'Everyone laughed at us,' they recount, 'despite the long history of grain growing in this area, people had this opinion that you couldn't grow decent milling wheat in damp Ceredigion.'

They managed to persuade friends near Aberystwyth, further up the coast, to grow some for them, and in 2009, with some trepidation, they milled the first crop of local grain. 'It was tasty – less strong than what you normally get, but tasty'. They started selling this flour locally as 'Ceredigion flour', and, before long, were milling 3 tonnes of it a year, and receiving good reports from their customers. Wheat grown under ideal conditions – somewhere like Canada or Russia, with cold winters and warm, dry summers – has a high protein content.[9] The British Isles, and particularly the more western parts, are more characteristically damp, and, although summers can be good, average daytime temperatures hover around 20C, even in low-lying parts. As a result, wheat grown in western Wales does not often come near the standards adhered to in commercial mills. But the Parrys wanted to get at this idea of 'terroir' in wheat. The same variety grown in Aberystwyth and Hertfordshire tastes different, and that should be reason enough to grow grain in different regions. Commercial mills typically mix wheat from different sources to meet the standards they have of protein content. 'But the beauty of what we do is that we can mill individual varieties of wheat from individual farmers. Every variety tastes different, and mills differently. And the exciting thing is, these days we have some bakers in Wales who are starting to explore all this potential again.'

In 2013, they got involved in setting up the Welsh Grain Forum, as a means of promoting local grain growing for use within Wales, drawing on the old history of grain growing in this country. The Forum is a voluntary networking group that brings together bakers, millers, thatchers, brewers and others to promote sustainable grain growing and real bread-making in Wales. One of the most exciting discoveries for the Forum was being approached in 2014 by a grain enthusiast from London, Andy Forbes, about the reintroduction of a traditional Welsh variety of wheat called 'Hen Gymro' – 'Old Welshman'.

The University of Wales dictionary of the Welsh language gives *c.*1850 as the oldest attested use of the word 'Hen Gymro' for a variety of wheat – although, as the name suggests, it is likely to go back much further than this. In southern England, traditional 'landraces' of wheat (local varieties of grain, adapted to prevailing conditions in their specific areas) had gone out of cultivation by the mid-19th century,[10] but farmers in western parts of Wales were still growing this traditional variety – despite encouragement to switch to more modern cultivars – as late as the 1930s.

Samples of 'Hen Gymro' were collected from farms near Lampeter from 1918 onwards by researchers from the Welsh plant breeding station near Aberystwyth, which was at the time led by the pioneering grassland scientist, George Stapledon. He described it as 'that well-known and essentially Welsh wheat'.[11] His researchers identified over 250 different sub-types of the variety – a remarkable degree of genetic diversity, which had probably contributed to its continuing resilience and usefulness to farmers. Their attention was drawn to it precisely because of the farmers' persistence in growing what the breeding station considered an antiquated variety, though they did add that 'it would be too much to assume that this preference [on the farmers' part] was due entirely to either ignorance or prejudice.'[12] After fieldwork on various farms, the researchers identified four possible reasons for the old landrace's survival:

* It was usually grown for home bread-making purposes.
* The conditions under which it was grown were usually unfavourable.
* The old variety, season by season, was better able to produce millable grain, particularly under adverse ripening conditions.
* The long, slender, and tough straw made first-rate thatching material.

Their ultimate conclusion was that Hen Gymro gives 'good quality grain under poor ripening conditions'. This is borne out by the accession register for November 1919, which mentions the names of some of the farms (Penlan, Frowen) from which the seed had come. The remarkable thing is that some of these farms were located above 250 metres, or 800 feet, above sea level – an altitude high enough to be substantially wetter than the valley floors in maritime Carmarthenshire or Ceredigion, and thus unfavourable for grain growing even by the standards of the time. In other words, this old landrace had a number of qualities that made it much more resilient as a crop than modern varieties of wheat, even if overall yields were generally lower. Over the course of the ensuing decades, Hen Gymro slowly fell out of use, until at some point in the mid-20th century the last field of it was sown and reaped somewhere in western Wales. Here is where the twist in this tale happens. By happy chance, some of the Hen Gymro seed found its way to the Vavilov Institute in St Petersburg. This institute was at the time collecting the world's largest bank of plant seeds, and it was common practice for institutions of this type to share seeds. And so, as Hen Gymro fell out of use in Wales, and St Petersburg suffered the Second World War and then years of communist rule, Hen Gymro seeds sat in climate-controlled conditions for decades, as it slowly fell from memory in its home territory.

Then, in 2011, some members of the Brockwell Bake association started growing Hen Gymro alongside some other old British wheat, using a strain of it known as 'S70', which had been preserved in other genebanks in both the UK and the Netherlands. In 2014, however, Andrew Whiteley, the real bread guru based in Scotland, was invited to St Petersburg and given some Hen Gymro seed to bring back to the UK with him. This, it turned out, was S72 Hen Gymro seed; genetically different to the 'S70' Hen Gymro and one of those selected by the Aberystwyth institute but later lost. More promisingly still, there was a further accession of seed containing at least five or six different types of Hen Gymro, giving a more genetically representative mix of the wheat as it would have been traditionally grown.

Andy Forbes and others who were part of Brockwell Bake grew the wheat and, over some years, had managed to bulk Hen Gymro up in London to a good amount of seed, and sent 15kg or so to the Welsh Grain Forum. From 2015 onwards, Hen Gymro was reintroduced to Wales. It was grown on several different sites, with the aim at each one to bulk up the seed. Interestingly, cropping was highly variable. In some cases, 10kg of seed produced 60kg by the end of the ensuing harvest. In other cases, it was all lost. But over the years, the volume of Hen Gymro has developed, and it has been grown in more and more locations in Wales, from St Davids to Builth Wells. 'The idea is to progress it to a marketable level,' explains Anne, 'and this year, we have even got it growing down the road from us again, at the National Trust place in Llanerchaeron.' Four acres of the wheat have been sown on those fields in the Aeron valley – where we know for certain that the variety was last grown in the 1930s.

Anne then whisks back the tea-towel that had been covering something on the farmhouse table where we'd been sitting and talking. Underneath was a walnut-coloured half-loaf of bread. That's when she made her irresistible offer: 'Would you like to try some Hen Gymro bread? It was baked four days ago, so it's a little stale … but you're welcome to try it.' And so there I was, eating this bread that had been baked in Felin Ganol, using wheat from the mill, grown with the old wheat landrace that had been collected 15 miles away from here in the early twentieth century and that had for centuries been the familiar flavour of bread – and most of all of *bara menyn* in this part of the world. I muse as I eat that bread – that most basic of foodstuffs for so much of the Western world – has enough history, culture and variety to endlessly fascinate both mind and palate.

In order to do justice to this endless bread potential, the challenge now, as Anne explains, is to resurrect an entire food system, such as used to exist, of grain growers, millers, bakers and customers. It's a question of resurrecting a cornerstone of the food economy, and creating the conditions for more people, in time, to earn their livelihoods locally from producing bread of the highest quality. Every part of this system needs to be moved on at the same time for it to really work and take root; it is useless creating capacity for milling, for instance, when there is no grain available locally to be milled, and no customer base for the flour and bread. But by the same token, growing more grain locally than can be milled means the farmer is taking a financial risk he or she can't justify.

The latent value of this sort of food economy to local people became abundantly clear when the Coronavirus pandemic hit in 2020. In March of that year, their phone began to ring and they found customers doubling their orders, new customers calling, the village shops that they supplied with a few bags of flour every month suddenly asking for 30 bags a week, and enquiries for flour coming in from all over the UK. They had plenty of water after a wet winter and so began milling every hour they could, drafting in the family to help with the packing. Working small and locally meant that the neighbouring farmer growing some of their grain could deliver readily. They could really see, suddenly, the difference it made to their community to have this hyperlocal source of good flour. In those first few weeks of the pandemic, they milled as much each week as they had been used to doing in a month.

The benefits of such a local bread economy also extend to people's health. Traditionally made bread using older landraces such as Hen Gymro has a much lower gluten content than conventional supermarket loaves. Part of the story – and perhaps the scandal – of bread in the Western world over the course of the last century is the enormous change in the gluten content of wheat, as wheat varieties have been bred for ever higher gluten content at the expense of other parts of the grain. Over the past ten years, the effects of this on human health have received increasing attention; there seems to be a causal link between this change and the increasing prevalence of gluten intolerance in Western populations. Talking to bakers about these changes bears out the observation: all have customers who tell them that they simply can't digest mass-produced conventional loaves, whereas slow-fermented loaves made with older grains such as spelt or barley doesn't produce symptoms. The increase in gluten content has also happened alongside a decrease in mineral content: US researchers tracked the nutrient profile of a range of wheat varieties over the last 130 years, and found that iron levels declined on average by 28% during this period, and zinc and selenium by roughly a third.[13] Put all this together, and you have a strong public health argument for investing in growing older, more nutritious varieties of wheat and widening the range of grains commonly eaten.

But even with all this in favour of *Hen Gymro* and the other grains milled at Felin Ganol, and with a dedicated local customer base, ten years in to the venture, the mill has only just paid for its own restoration, and isn't yet turning in a profit. 'Our hope is to be able to pass this on as a viable concern to someone else when we finish', says Anne. Felin Ganol currently mills grain from four different suppliers: a farmer near Builth, a farm in the Vale of Glamorgan, Moelifor in Llanrhystud itself (their neighbouring farmer was finally persuaded to put down some five acres to grain for them right next door) and then farmers in Shropshire, just over the border. In future, the hope and dream is that an ever greater percentage of this grain will be grown locally. But, from the start, they have focused on milling the same diversity of grains as was the case at the mill in times past.

Currently, they mill wheat, barley and rye, almost all of which is organically grown. And although they sell their flour retail at the farm door and wholesale to delis in the area, it's in supplying local bakers that they see the future. They currently supply five bakers with flour, all of which are in mid-Wales, in an arc with Llanrhystud at its centre, from Machynlleth around to Llanidloes, Abergavenny, Lampeter and Cardigan. All of these people are making real bread, and some of them are really exploring the potential that using different varieties of wheat or other grains gives, bringing out the flavour and terroir. As Anne puts it, 'the thing with milling as we do it here is that we can mill a specific variety, grown in a particular field and year, and tell you where it's from'.

Baking the bread

One of the bakers at the heart of this revival is Andy, of 'Andy's Bread' in Llanidloes, a town of 3,000 nestled in the hills of mid-Wales, whom I visit on a dull summer's day. He started baking in 2010, using his home oven and growing his business gradually to the point where it now employs three people, baking two hundred loaves a day, five days a week. 'We could grow the business further,' he explains, 'but I wanted us to stay as a small, local bakery serving this town. When a new bakery opened in Machynlleth over the mountain, they told me out of courtesy, almost apologising for it. But I was glad; why do I want to be going over the mountain to Machynlleth? Much better that there's a bakery in the town there, supplying the locals with good bread!' There used to be three bakeries in Llanidloes, Andy explains. One of his customers brought him an old baking tin from one of the old town bakeries, a tin that had in all likelihood not been used in over thirty years. When Andy started selling bread locally, there wasn't another bakery in the entire area.

Originally from the Wirral, Andy is more fervent a proponent of Welsh produce and supporting the rural Welsh economy than most natives. His sourdough bread has only three essential ingredients: flour, water and salt. Local water is easy, as the tap water that comes from these hills is the same quality as many bottled waters. For pastries and croissants, Andy uses organic butter from a farmers' co-operative in Carmarthenshire, Calon Wen. For focaccia, Hafod Cheese is the product of choice. For salt, he has been testing Halen Môn. The flour was the greater challenge.

Shipton Mill in Gloucestershire not far over the English border provides good quality baking flour, and Andy became a regular customer. But when Felin Ganol came along, it opened up the possibility of baking a loaf using flour milled within a few dozen miles. 'It's been great seeing it develop. There's a real connection, you know what you've got. It makes a tastier loaf than roller milled flour, no doubt about that. But it's also been a learning experience for me as a baker. Because of the stone-milling, the flour is that bit coarser and its water-absorption isn't the same as it is with your standard bread flour from a big mill. But then you also realize that it varies – just a little – month by month. So as a baker you adapt and learn. I like working with it, ultimately I think it makes a tasty loaf.'

Andy is looking forward to baking with Hen Gymro flour in the future, which he hasn't had much chance to use yet. 'That'll be a fun challenge too. When you're working with these lower-protein grains, as most of the old ones are, they do make less "fluffy", denser loaves. So you play around with them, learn techniques that I daresay the old bakers knew as second-nature.'

His loaves are all given distinctive names: the 'Ceredigion', using some of Felin Ganol's wholemeal flour and so reflecting its county of origin; 'Llani Wild', a sourdough reflecting the locals' nickname for the town; and 'Dolly' from the name of the local housing co-operative where he first baked. I take some Llani Wild home with me, and have a slice with butter. This is *bara menyn* as it should be, the soft fat of the butter coating a crumb that has that elasticity and mouth-filling grain-ness that only real bread has. It is immensely moreish, in a way that makes me reflect on how good bread and butter can form a satisfying, frugal meal that a mass-produced loaf and margarine simply can't.

A few months later and August is upon us, with its customary mix (at least in western Wales) of sunshine, showers and the occasional early autumn storm. One of those, with winds of up to 50 mph around western coasts, had hit a few days before I visited Llanerchaeron to see how the field of Hen Gymro from St Petersburg had grown. Paul, the farmer on this National Trust estate, takes me to the six-acre field where the crop was growing. 'Here it is,' he says, as we walk into a field full of wheat as tall as a man, 'it's the first time anyone has seen this growing in Wales for over 70 years! You're lucky – we would have harvested it a few days ago, but as soon as I bring the thresher to the field gate, there's another shower.'

The crop is marvellous chunky ears of wheat on long, thin, rust-coloured legs. Paul's enthusiasm for it is infectious; 'You know, when I was reading up about the strain of Hen Gymro growing here, they always talk about its reddish tinge. Well, it grew all the way through spring, all the way through the June and July heat without so much as a hint of red. Then suddenly, not two weeks ago it took on this distinct rust-red hue!'

He's animated: 'It really has been fascinating to grow. I only sowed it at half density, and I was sure it would be choked with the weeds. This field it's in was pasture, see, so we'd just ploughed this up and have been growing the crop entirely organically. Now, normally if you sow a field of organic modern wheat around here, your crop is going to be smothered with the vigorous summer growth we get in this climate. But look at it! This crop is entirely clean! And actually, when I read back in the descriptions of this, that's how it grew back in the day. The Aberystwyth researchers explicitly mention how this one just smothers the weeds, and that's exactly what it's done.'

I reflect on what Paul has said, as I learn later from the Parrys that Hen Gymro can't be grown at Llanerchaeron again next year.[14]

The Hen Gymro strains that have been preserved all these years provide a viable and useful crop of wheat for these parts that grow well with zero to no input, on land generally classed as marginal. It can then be milled in places like Felin Ganol, using no electricity whatsoever, and made into delicious (lower gluten) bread. In other words, this is a way of growing grain and milling flour in Wales in the future, in a way that is sustainable, doesn't damage the land, is better for people's guts and uses very little carbon. As part of a grain economy including bakers as well, it might also prove to be a better source of rural income and employment than the current dominant model in Wales – and indeed beyond.

Paul finishes telling me about the Hen Gymro before rushing off to other farm jobs. His parting shot is telling: 'What's more, if you think back to the gales we had at the weekend, I thought the next morning I'd come here and it would all be flat. But no, it's withstood it all, almost as though it were designed for that type of weather.'

2

CAWS / CHEESE

'In glorious weather the sixth annual cheese show is underway at the commodious Market Hall, Caerphilly. As early as eight o'clock the town began to assume a busy appearance, and as the day wore on visitors from far and near, availing themselves of the summery weather, came pouring in. Caerphilly cheese, once the typical Welsh cheese, but having been superseded by Dutch and American products, has of late been more generally sought after, to the consequent benefit of the district. This happy result has been due to the spirited action of David Lewis, Bronrhiw, who has just secured a recognized trade mark for this make of cheese. This trade mark will be duly registered, and no cheese in the future, unless it bears the registered imprint, will be genuine Caerphilly. The characteristic feature of the trademark is a device – the famous leaning tower of Caerphilly Castle – and the words *Caws Cymru, caws pur* ("Welsh cheese, pure cheese") surrounded in bold lettering by "Caerphilly Cheese".'

Thus begins the report in *The Merthyr Times* on the annual Caerphilly Cheese Show of 3 October 1895, showcasing one of Wales's most emblematic foodstuffs: cheese. Caerphilly cheese is only the most prominent survivor in the modern era of a cheese heritage that from early on both shaped perceptions of the Welsh – Welsh rarebit as glorified cheese on toast, for example – and also brought in good money for a quality product. Cheese making in Wales goes back as far as our records go, and has always been a prominent foodstuff, remarked upon by native writers and outside observers alike. By the 18th century, with cheese finally growing in popularity in England too, it also became a commodity. Many towns across Wales, from Hay-on-Wye in the borderlands to Harlech on the west coast, developed cheese markets (and in both those towns, the fine market buildings still stand) but the one at Caerphilly stands out.

As early as 1833, cheese was listed as being one of the three principal 'articles exposed for sale' at Caerphilly market.[1] As production and demand grew, so did the town market's reputation for cheese. As an 1890s newspaper exposé revealed, cheese from other counties started to be pirated into the county under the guise of Caerphilly cheese. It was in order to combat this cheese fraudulence that the standing committee of the market adopted the brand with the *Caws Cymru, caws pur* motto and insignia showing the leaning tower.[2] In order to further buttress the cheese's reputation, it was graded and stamped from the 1890s[3] at specific cheese fairs held in a new purpose-built market hall, which employed an official cheese taster.[4] Cheese fairs were held in the market hall in April, July, August, October and November each year, as well as the annual cheese show each September.[5] The second half of the 19th century was thus the heyday of Caerphilly cheese, with brisk trading, high quality and a burgeoning market.

By around 1910, however, the seeds of a downturn had already been sown. Many local farmers stopped production as they found it more lucrative to sell milk to the booming port of Cardiff a few miles away. At some point in the following decade, in a dramatic reversal of fortune for Caerphilly, the market hall closed. Local farms continued production, selling Caerphilly cheese directly to local grocers in the area and beyond until the late 1930s. But commercial production was then brought to an abrupt halt with the outbreak of the Second World War by order of the Ministry of Agriculture, as the first priority decided by central government at Westminster was liquid milk. Some cheeses, including both Cheddar and Cheshire, were permitted to be made as they had a longer shelf life, but the ban on Caerphilly was not lifted until 1954.

Cheese country

The Englishman, Nathaniel Crouch, recorded a ditty from the borderlands of north-eastern Wales during his travels around the country in 1695:

'They have cheese very tender and palatable, the pedigree thereof
     was by one airily derived:
Adam's nawn Cusson was by her Birth
Ap Curds, ap Milk, ap Cow, ap Grass, ap Earth'

The ditty plays on the old Welsh penchant for genealogies, with 'ap' being the equivalent of the ubiquitous Gaelic 'mac'. 'Cusson' is here most likely a corruption of *cosyn*, the Welsh for 'a cheese' or 'a block of cheese'. So we have here a bilingual witticism, giving the full genealogy of cheese all the way back to its ancestor, Earth, via the grass, the cow, the milk and the curds. Despite the comic intent, this is in many ways an appropriate way to ground cheese in both the land and culture of Wales. The Atlantic seaboard of

Europe from Asturias in Spain up to Northern Ireland is prime grass country, with a mild climate and plentiful rainfall. Wales sits on this arc, warmed and wetted by the Gulf Stream. Perfect conditions, in short, for cheese to become an important food.

The human palate can distinguish five flavours – sweet, sour, bitter, salty and savoury. Almost uniquely, cheese can deliver all five, which perhaps goes some way to explain its universal popularity in those societies where the right growing and genetic conditions coincide (not all humans can easily digest the milk sugar, lactose – historically limiting the importance of dairy in many societies). But the degree to which cheese as a foodstuff became associated with the Welsh goes further than what mere geography and genetics can account for. From Welsh rarebit to Caerphilly cheese, cheese has long been seen by outsiders (often English) as one of the foods most characteristic of the Welsh.

The highest point in Wales is the peak of *Yr Wyddfa* – Snowdon, as the Vikings baptized it from their sea-ships. Crowned for years by a dismal concrete bunker of a café that served the almost half a million people that visit the summit each year, it was replaced in 2009 by a new visitor centre called *Hafod Eryri*. The element *hafod* – summer abode – is found in place-names across the country, particularly down its mountainous central spine. Together with the *hendre* – winter abode – they form two halves of the old system known as transhumance that shaped so much of Welsh society down the ages, in common with mountainous areas across Europe, and that survived in parts into the twentieth century.

When the first grass started growing in the high places after the winter ice and snow had passed, a few workers from each farm would go up to their summer abode high up in the hills, taking the cows, sheep and goats with them. There was a set date for this, shared with the Gaelic cultures of Ireland and Scotland: *Calan Mai*, or May day. As the flocks and herds fattened up on the abundant new growth and the flow of milk increased, others, including the women of the families, would come up from the valley farms to join them. During those long summer days, the women would work together to bring forth from the milky abundance a product that would keep through the dark winter days to come, churning, washing, salting butter, and above all, making cheese. When *Calan Gaeaf*, 31 October, arrived, it would be time to return to the winter dwellings in the valleys to sit out the winter dark and cold – with the growth of summer condensed into rounds of fragrant cheese.

The roots of this practice go back in all likelihood to the arrival of the first farmers in Wales during the Neolithic period, around 4000 BC.[6] It had survived with probably little alteration into the 12th century, when the contemporary observer Gerald of Wales noted that 'almost all the population lives on its flocks and on oats, milk, cheese and butter'. The native body of Welsh law, 'Cyfraith Hywel', mentions cheese washed in brine as one of the possessions that a divorced woman was entitled to keep. Other contemporary records, from both Wales and neighbouring parts of the British Isles confirm the surmise that women were usually the ones that made cheese. We have a more detailed description of the practice by an onlooker, the antiquarian Thomas Pennant, who describes life in the *hafod* in his day in the second half of the eighteenth century: 'This mountainous tract scarcely yields any corn. Its produce is cattle and sheep, which, during summer, keep very high in the mountains, followed by their owners, with their families, who reside in that season in Hafodtai or summer dairy houses as the farmers do in the Swiss Alps in their "sennes". During summer, the men pass their time either in harvest work or in tending their herds; the women in milking or making butter and cheese. For their own uses, they milk both ewes and goats, and make cheese of the milk for their own consumption.'

This pattern, of summer cheese-making in the hills carried out by the womenfolk while the men tended to the flocks, continued well into the twentieth century, when oatcakes and cheese still formed the mainstay of hill folks' diet in the uplands of Wales as they had for many centuries.[7] As William Camden describes in his *Britannia* four hundred years after Gerald, the people of Merionethshire in his day 'for most part wholy betake themselves to breeding and seeding of cattail, and live upon white meates, as butter, cheese &c.'[8] Word of this Welsh predilection for cheese had obviously got to the chattering classes of England by the early sixteenth century, giving us this anecdote by the writer Andrew Boorde (d. 1549):

> It is written among old jests how God made St Peter porter of heaven ... at [one time] there was in heaven a great company of Welshmen which with their babbeling troubled all the others. Wherefore God said to St Peter that he was weary of them and he would love to have them out of heaven. To this St Peter said, 'Good Lord, I warrant you that shall shortly be done.' Wherefore St Peter went outside of heaven's gates and cried with a loud voice, 'Cause Babe! Cause Babe,' that is as much as to say 'Roasted Cheese!' Upon hearing this, the Welshmen ran out of heaven at a great pace ... and when St Peter saw them all out he suddenly went into heaven and locked the door – and so got all the Welshmen out!

Caws bob (or *caws bobi*) is the native term for what came to be known in English as Welsh rarebit. There are references to roasted cheese being a Welsh favourite from among all the different ways of eating cheese as early as medieval times,[9] and despite some controversy as to the English name for the dish (is it a Welsh *rabbit*? What is a rare-bit, anyway?), there is no serious dispute that the origins of this now endlessly variable dish lie in the Welsh love of cheese on toast, nor that cooked cheese was hardly known as a feature of English or continental diets. English cookbooks of the period omitted cheese entirely, and the German traveller, Carl Moritz, dismissed the dish as quite unpalatable.[10] Later dishes involving melted cheese on toast, such as the French 'croque-monsieur' are not mentioned until centuries later ('croquet-monsieur' itself only turning up on a Paris menu in 1910). This, then, was a Welsh particularity, and a notably long-lived one.

Older recipes from Wales are few and far between but one of the earliest comes from one of the first mass cookbooks in English, *The Art of Cookery* by Hannah Glasse of London, published in 1747. The recipe is placed next to a similar one for 'Scotch rabbit', which conspicuously lacks mustard:

To make a Scotch rabbit, toast the bread very nicely on both sides, butter it, cut a slice of cheese about as big as the bread, toast it on both sides, and lay it on the bread.

To make a Welsh rabbit, toast the bread on both sides, then toast the cheese on one side, lay it on the toast, and with a hot iron brown the other side. You may rub it over with mustard.

References to Welsh rarebit crop up repeatedly in dictionaries and cookbooks from across the British Isles and beyond over the ensuing century and a half, in ever more divergent forms, including some made with Béchamel sauce, Worcester sauce and paprika.

But there is no doubt that, while Welsh rarebit gained its fame in the taverns of London, North America and beyond, *caws bobi* continued to be used and enjoyed in Wales. Minwel Tibbott included two recipes from different parts of northern Wales in her 'Welsh fare', one of which includes beer. The English food writer Dorothy Hartley published in 1954 an old recipe that she had obtained from a certain Mrs Jones, which is typical of the dish by the early 20th century:

A teaspoonful of cornflour, two ounces of cheese
A teacup of milk, an ounce of butter
A quarter teaspoon of mustard, salt and pepper mixed,
   to season

Slice the cheese, melt the butter and mix with the cornflour, add the milk and cheese and seasoning to this, stir on a moderate heat until it is soft, and thickens. Pour on buttered, toasted bread and eat whilst warm.

Interestingly and typically, however, Mrs Jones does not here specify what type of cheese should be used. Did she have cow's cheese in mind, or perhaps goat or ewe's cheese? And are we here talking about a soft or a hard cheese – very different ingredients in cooking? And most crucially, does she have a particular named cheese in mind, and, if so, what was it called?

Welsh cheeses

The search for historical named cheeses in Wales, much like the search for the names of traditional fruit or vegetable varieties, runs quickly adrift in the moorless marshes of historical indifference to these things. Despite a wealth of records on common foods and food habits in Wales spanning the period from the 9th century to the 19th, very few of these accounts go beyond the generic in their description. But despite this, the outlines of Welsh cheese history can be traced with some certainty, and they shed light both on *caws bobi* and the modern predominance of Caerphilly among Welsh cheeses.

Part of the reason why a country with as important and varied a cheese tradition as Wales emerged in the twentieth century on the far side of industrialization with only one named cheese – Caerphilly – has to do precisely with the love of *caws bobi* and the resultant hankering after hard cheese. Apart from some narrow bands in the lowlands of the south and north-east, much of the hilly land of Wales is acidic in nature. This naturally produces cow's milk more suited to making soft cheeses – which are no good for Welsh rarebit – than well-matured hard cheeses. On top of this, the dietary and economic value of butter was generally higher than that of cheese, with the consequence that fat was generally skimmed off the top of cow's milk in order to create butter, with cheese then made from the leftover skimmed milk.[11] The thoroughness of the skimming process thus dictated the quality of the cow's cheese in a great many cases, with more thoroughly skimmed cheese (*caws llaeth glas*) again being of little use for Welsh rarebit.

Using sheep's (or in some cases goat's) cheese was one way around these issues, and a traveller to Wales in 1799 specifically mentions 'hard cheese' as being a core part of the diet in upland Merionethshire: '[Their] diet is not contemptible – oaten cake, or bread made by a mixture of wheat and rye, hard cheese, potatoes and excellent butter-milk, furnish a meal substantial and whole-some.'[12] Some of the traditional Welsh breeds of sheep, such as the Llanwenog and Llŷn sheep are known to produce good, fat- and protein-rich milk, and were historically bred for their milk. Native *caws bobi* is therefore likely in most cases historically to have been made with sheep's cheese, or an admixture of sheep and cow's cheese like the Greek halloumi. But cow's cheese was always more highly prized, and as a result, the Welsh from early on made efforts to trade – and then produce – the hard cheese of neighbouring parts of England. In the south-east, that meant Cheddar, and in the north-east, Cheshire.[13]

Cheshire is first mentioned by Thomas Muffet of London around 1580. By the mid-18th century it had become so popular, and production had increased to such an extent that the Royal Navy ordered its ships be stocked with it. By 1823, production had grown to 10,000 tonnes per year. Not all of this was made in Cheshire, however. The economic opportunities provided by Cheshire-making meant that by this period production had spread into neighbouring parts of north-eastern Wales, in particular Denbighshire and Flintshire with less acid soil than the rest of northern Wales, and the cheese had also become associated with this region.

Originally, Cheshire had been a pale golden colour, and was imitated by Welsh farmers who had started making a cheese in this style. The Welsh Cheshires were, unsurprisingly, often made with an admixture of goat's milk; this hybrid cheese started to be sold to coach passengers in the 19th century, bringing the Cheshire cheese brand into disrepute. The Welsh Cheshire producers were thus obliged by the authorities to add annatto – a naturally occurring food colouring used in cheese from the 16th century – to their cheese to mark them out. But, in a twist of fate, travellers and customers soon refused to believe that white Cheshire was indeed Cheshire, and so all Cheshire became coloured.[14] How much of this is long-standing rancour between the Welsh and the English is hard to ascertain; what is certain, however, is that by the mid-19th century, Cheshire made on Welsh farms had become in many cases a quality product and was recognized as such. The Cheshire made by Williams Jones of Fferm Pistyll, near Mold in north-eastern Wales, for example, won first prize in the Royal Agricultural Show of Liverpool, Manchester and North Cheshire in the year of the Show's anniversary in 1867.[15] Cheshire continued to be widely produced across north-eastern Wales for decades until the introduction of strict regulation of cheeses during the Second World War, which also spelt the death knell for many English and Scottish farmhouse cheeses as it pushed farmers away from cheese production.

By the close of the twentieth century, the only Welsh farmhouse producer still making Cheshire was the Latham family of Knolton farm of Overton, near Wrexham.[16] The Lathams have roots on both sides of the border, and on Robert Latham's side, generations in the Overton area itself. An ancestor of his, Robert Latham (who died in April 1733) was recorded as owning at that time:

* 10 heads of cattle worth £30.0.0p
* Cheese press worth 18.0p
* Package of cheese worth 18.0.0p

The family has owned the present farm since 1940, and production today continues in the hands of Jonathan Latham and sons Scott and Stuart, who once again sell their white Cheshire at local markets and delis.

Cheshire was never made in other parts of the country, however. The hard cheese tradition in south-eastern Wales is also shared with neighbouring parts of England, namely that of Cheddar-making.

Cheddar, first made in the Somerset village of the same name, is recorded as a distinct cheese as early as the 12th century.[17] The village lies on limestone ground (so non-acidic) in the shadow of the Mendip hills, from the tops of which the coast of Glamorgan can clearly be seen less than 20 miles distant. A hard cheese, matured for many months, Cheddar was widely desired in southern Wales for *caws bobi*, and over time also made in farms along the southern coastal belt of lime-rich soils for sale in the industrial towns. By the early 20th century, two cheeses were commonly available in town markets in southern Wales – Caerphilly (for which housewives were willing to pay a premium)[18] or cheddar, commonly known as 'American'. This was often a mild cheese, but stronger more authentic stuff was preferred when available. The modern Welsh Collier's brand of cheddar, made in Denbighshire today and widely sold in supermarkets throughout the UK, is based on this tradition, and quotes in its marketing literature the miners' preference for strong cheddar or Caerphilly for their lunch packs. By the 1960s, with the growth of the Milk Marketing Board, which controlled cheese production, industrial or creamery produced Welsh 'cheddar' cheese was lumped together with English cheese. By that point, the dominance of creameries and the specialization of agriculture in Wales meant that two-thirds of all the creamy cheese produced in England and Wales was made in Wales – the vast majority of it Cheddar.

With more than a little historical basis then, we can claim both Cheshire and Cheddar as historical Welsh cheeses – with at least as much justification as many other national specialities worldwide, which on closer inspection are not as native as sometimes made out (English tea or Italian tomatoes, anyone?). But the Welsh cheese most strongly associated with the country is of course Caerphilly itself.

Caws Caerffili

Commentators in the early 19th century were united in noting that the dominant cattle breeds of southern Wales tended to produce better milch cows than those of northern Wales, which tended to be beef or store cattle. C. S. Reed, writing in 1849, describes the black Pembrokeshire cow as being 'an excellent milch cow that gives 10 quarts a day of fatty milk'.[19] The native breed of south-eastern Wales, where the town of Caerphilly is located, were the brown Glamorgan cattle, which produced excellent milk cows, well able to supply the growing industrial towns of those parts.[20] From these cows a hard, mild, quick-maturing cheese was made, sometimes known in English as 'Glamorgan cheese', and in Welsh as *cosyn cnap*.[21]

This cheese was historically made also with ewe's milk. John Evans, visiting Glamorgan in 1804, describes the Ewenny and St Fagans ewe's cheeses of the southern, lowland parts of the county: 'A kind of cheese is made in some parts of the country of all sheeps' milk, or a mixture of sheep and cows' milk, exceedingly rich and highly flavoured; and when of a proper age, little if at all inferior to the boasted Parmesan. That made at Ewenny sells at one shilling per pound, while that of the dairies about St Fagans brings 16 pence.'[22] There was thus variation across southern Wales in the cheese that was made, and much of this variation would have been even between individual farms. This tradition – a farmhouse tradition, naturally – was the forerunner to what became known as Caerphilly.

The industrialization and concurrent urbanization in the second half of the nineteenth century created a much expanded market for cheeses amongst the urban middle-classes and poor. As a result, more successful cheeses across Britain and beyond started to be widely named and known by name as they were exported and marketed. The name 'Caerphilly', that of the old market town cum-coal mining town some ten miles north of Cardiff, was thus given to this regional cheese, despite production continuing on numerous small-scale farms in other parts of Glamorgan, Monmouthshire and neighbouring parts of southern Wales between the 1800s and the 1930s.[23] The town's markets and fairs were thus responsible for this new epithet for Glamorgan cheese, which quickly became a favourite of miners across the coal valleys of southern Wales for its classic hard cheese combination of good flavour and good storage properties when working underground. With the opening of the cheese market and the new brand, Caerphilly had its moment in the sun, being produced to a consistent and high standard and available across southern Wales and beyond.

But beyond the hum of buying and selling at markets, the Glamorgan cheese farmhouse tradition continued across the southern half of Wales and particularly in rural areas far removed from the industrial communities, the cheese making practices had undergone little if any change as a result of Caerphilly's stand-ardization. The windswept Epynt hills of Brecknockshire, within a couple of hours' journey to Caerphilly by car, were taken over by the British Army in 1939, and the Welsh-speaking farming commu-nities who lived there forcibly removed from their ancestral lands without fair compensation. One of the farming wives in these hills, Mrs Ceinwen Davies of Fferm Gwybedog, was a cheesemaker, who made Caerphilly-style cheese for domestic use and to sell at the mar-ket in Llanwrtyd or the November Brecon Fair. Her cheese-making methods were recorded: she would mix a gallon of ewe's milk with two gallons of cows' milk, one of which would be skimmed. The cheese would be left to mature for at least two months, but often up to six months.[24] It thus seems likely that the Welsh sheep's cheese tradition, in Caerphilly form, lasted well into the middle decades of the twentieth century in areas like this. Traditions continued long in rural parts – entire villages in the Welsh countryside were not connected to the electricity grid until the 1960s, many decades after the large towns and cities.

Despite the variation arising from widespread farmhouse production, Caerphilly cheese itself was generally known as a small, round cheese – much smaller than Cheshire, which weighed 60–80lb.[25] One of its main features was its speed to mature – from four days to four months, with a longer aging process leading to a higher quality cheese. If stored beyond this – and many farms did keep some back for themselves, leaving it to mature for up to nine months – the cheese would develop a creamy fragrance and blue veins, much as in Stilton-type cheeses. A good Caerphilly has a mottled rind and a distinctive mild, lemony flavour. This is a hard cheese that veers towards the crumbly end of the spectrum. Not particularly good therefore for a Welsh rarebit (hence the Cheddar) but delightful paired with fruit or eaten by itself. As the World Cheese book puts it, 'Caerphilly has a delicious fresh taste and sometimes, when the grazing is at its best, its usual herbaceous sweetness is infused as with a rustic béchamel sauce by the scent of crushed bracken moistened by autumnal rains. With age, it becomes softer, creamier and more supple as it grows a blueish grey coat, which sometimes sneaks onto the surface of the cheese and indicates it is still alive and well.'[26]

Caws Cenarth

Today, there are three artisan Caerphilly cheese makers in Wales, two of which are in the lush Teifi valley of south-western Wales.

This land has long been praised for its rich pastures, and the long grass growing season means that it remains prime cattle country. Salmon continue to travel up the Teifi river to spawn, jumping the rapids and falls at the beauty spot of Cenarth. Some two miles south of here, in the valley of the river Cych, lies Fferm Glyneithinog, the home of Wales's arguably best-known cheesemaker today, Caws Cenarth.

The company is indelibly associated with the stamp of its founder, Thelma Adams, now retired, who established this farmhouse cheese company in 1986 at a time when newly-introduced milk quotas were driving many other farmers in western Wales out of business. The fact that cheese making was an accepted part of life for this farmer's daughter from the Carmarthenshire hills is far from being sufficient explanation for the extraordinary success and visibility the company has enjoyed since it was established. Bold marketing – including writing in their second year to the procurement managers of both Harrods and Selfridges in London – was essential for that. But to land on those shelves, the cheese itself needed to be of quality – and the Caerphilly-making tradition Thelma was born into was the reason for that.

Thelma's grandfather had been a dairy farmer, and her parents continued the tradition on the smallholding on which she grew up during the war years – with plentiful supplies of home-made cheese and butter from her parents' two cows, Seren and Blackie. Her mother made a soft, crumbly Caerphilly from the leftover milk whenever the cows were producing well, and she remembered how her father would punch holes in large corn beef tins in order to make cheese moulds. 'Often, we children would creep into the pantry when the adults weren't watching and would help ourselves to big chunks of the delicious cheese', she reminisces.[27] And Thelma had continued making cheese for her family as an adult – small batches of Caerphilly-style cheese made from memory.

So when new milk quotas were introduced in April 1984, driving many dairy farmers out of business very quickly, Thelma and her husband, Gwynfor, looked around for alternative ways of using the milk. The cheese-making tradition in the family, along with Thelma's enjoyment of the process, provided the starting point; a competition run by the regional development agency for mid-Wales provided initial capital of £5,000, and the generally poor quality of creamery-produced Caerphilly sold at the time provided the openings of a market. A search for traditional cheese presses up and down the lanes of Carmarthenshire and Ceredigion ensued. Historically, there had been both Carmarthen and Cardigan-type cheese presses, but many farmers – like Gwynfor's own parents – had thrown theirs out over the middle decades of the twentieth century with the (heavily subsidized) modernization of agriculture. Usable ones were found, including in the closing down sale of an old creamery in Carmarthen itself. Cheese was made, trialled, improved and on 2 April 1987, Caws Cenarth was launched, making traditional, unpasteurized Caerphilly – made by hand by Thelma Adams with milk from the farm herd.

Many marketing pushes, several awards and tonnes of cheese followed over the next decade and a half, and, in 2005, their son Carwyn took over the business. He and his Russian wife, Susanna, were already highly involved, having developed a few years previously both Perl Wen and Perl Las – soft cheeses, the former Brie-like and the latter a blue cheese – which were almost instant successes, and novelties on the Welsh scene. He explains to me that they had to make the difficult decision to sell the dairy herd his father had built up, and rent out their organic pasture land to neighbouring farmers, because it wasn't feasible to continue growing the cheese business and farm well. They now buy in their milk from a couple of local farmers, including relatives of theirs, all within a 20-mile radius.

I ask what the company's long-term goals are, now that they are purely a cheese-making outfit. Carwyn's answer is instantaneous: 'We want to grow the business so that people import less cheese from the continent. That's our competition – high-end French cheeses. We want to grow the market here in Wales and in the UK so that we can in turn create a market for all our neighbours' milk.' It transpires later on in our conversation that Caws Cenarth doesn't export (other than on demand to individual customers, for precisely this reason. Carwyn is obviously animated by a vision where cheese-eaters and buyers in Wales and beyond know their local cheeses, know who made them, and buy them locally. That the farm is open to visitors six days a week, with a shop and exhibition on site is testament to this; its location, several miles from a main road and away from the tourist traps of the coast, means that this represents only a small fraction of their business. And unlike many food companies of this size (25 employees), everyone at Caws Cenarth is a cheesemaker – there are no specific marketing or sales staff. Teaching the public about cheese making and where the food comes from is clearly a value that Carwyn holds dear.

This comes out again as he muses on conflicting customer demands. 'On the one hand, you have this strong movement against plastic – which I get. And if people were willing to go to their farmer's market, or even supermarket with containers and buy off the block, that'd be great. And it would save us money on packaging. But then on the other hand, we see this trend where people actually want their cheese in smaller packages, 250g instead of 500g. And they want long shelf life; they don't realize that the cheese we make has an entirely natural life-cycle, and it does reach a peak and then decline. Actually, one of the things we're thinking of introducing is a clock on the packaging, where it shows over time if the cheese is slightly less mature, fully mature, over mature and so on. But there is this constant battle where customers – and supermarkets – want absolute uniformity, consistency, predictability. But we are in the business of making something artisanal, with lots of variables, like the time of year. Lots of continental cheesemakers standardize their milk for uniformity using a complex method of removing the fats and proteins then reblending, which we don't do. And everything we make is still made by hand; our Golden Cenarth, for instance, is handled an average of 12–15 times during ripening.'

The other aspect that Carwyn is keen to develop is the breeds of cattle used for the cheeses. They already do make cheese from milk that comes from a single, often heritage breed of cow. But the different fat and protein composition that different breeds produce (such as the well-known high fat content of Jersey cattle) gives the potential for bringing out fine differences in flavour and texture in the cheese – and making an excellent cheese into an exceptional one. And it's not just overall fat levels, but even the size of the fat globules themselves that matter here.[28] Cheese made with small milk fat globule milk retains more salt and contains more moisture than it otherwise would, while cheese made with larger milk fat globule milk lends itself more readily to toasting. Overall, small milk fat globules produce a better cheese structure that can be aged on longer, whilst cheese made with large fat globules are better suited to producing creamier and softer cheeses.

In many ways, as I observe to Carwyn, he is simply returning to a default that traditional cheesemakers in Wales worked with out of necessity. They made Caerphilly because the traditional breeds and the soil acidity levels led to milk that lent itself to making that kind of cheese. He is in a position where he can make the choice to use those breeds and that kind of milk, in order to bring out those characteristics that led to the development of Caerphilly in the first place. 'It's funny you should say that,' Carwyn interjects, 'because we're also working on using more ewes' milk, like they used to in Wales – and using mixtures of sheep and cows' milk together to make cheese.'

He takes me out and across the farmyard, and reaches for a round of cheese that was sat on the shelf, maturing. 'Oh! Look at this. The rind has gone even darker than I thought! This is a test-batch, cow and sheep's cheese mixed together. Let's have a taste now.' He cuts into it, holds it up to the light for me to see the texture, and then gives me a piece. It is delicious – tangy and mild at the same time, with the strength of the ewe's cheese giving it a firmer, much less crumbly texture than a classic modern Caerphilly, but retaining that light, lemony flavour. I am sold – and tell him so.

'... salted herrings are almost the only fish they eat,
for although they live close to the sea, they seldom take
the trouble to procure it, yet they are remarkably partial
to cockles.'

E. Donovan, 1805

3

LAWR, COCOS
AC WYSTRYS /
LAVER, COCKLES AND OYSTERS

orphyra umbilicalis, Bara lawr, 'the Welshman's caviar',
'Laverbread'. A dark green – or is it red? – or pink or deep
brown?[1] – seaweed that is simultaneously the crowning joy and
sharpest point of division of all Welsh foods. Crowning joy, because
this is a true delicacy, with a deep umami flavour and a rich, smooth
texture that fills your mouth.[2] Sharp point of division, because, like
Marmite, this is a love-it-or-hate-it foodstuff, shunned and adored
in equal measure even within the same family.

Laverbread, properly speaking, is the finished product made
with laver, the name of the seaweed itself, derived from the Latin
laver, laveris and cognate with the Welsh 'lawr'. It is native to
rocks on all the westward shores of the British Isles, grows best in
cold nitrogen-rich water, is one of the major plant-based sources of
vitamin B12, and has a high content of a number of dietary minerals, with concentrations of both iron and iodine particularly high
(the iodine is what gives it the characteristic umami flavour akin to

oysters or olives).[3] And its marine riches have been appreciated for a long time in Wales.

We don't know exactly when people first started harvesting and using laver in this part of the British Isles, but Gerald of Wales mentions its use in Pembrokeshire in the 12th century. At Freshwater West on the southern coast, women collected the seaweed from the rocks and hung it up in huts.[4] William Camden, writing in his volume *Britannia* in 1607 gives us a more detailed account of how the weed was harvested in springtime: 'Near St Davids, especially at Eglwys Abernon, and in many other places along the Pembrokeshire Coast, the peasantry gather in the Spring time a kind of Alga or seaweed, where they made a sort of food called llavan or llawvan, in English, black butter. The seaweed is washed clean from the sand, and sweated between two tile stones. The weed is then shred small and well-kneaded, as they do dough for bread, and made up into great balls or rolls, which some eat raw, and others fry with oatmeal and butter'.[5]

In more recent times, and certainly by the early 19th century, a cottage industry had grown up on the Burry Inlet and the Loughor estuary between Gower and Llanelli, and laver was a mainstay at nearby Swansea market. A Victorian writer describing the curiosities of south Wales records that the laver on the southern Gower coast was gathered 'close to low-watermark, washed well in sea water to free it from sand, then boiled 12 hours and seasoned with salt'. Being easily harvestable, it provided welcome pocket money to poorer people in coastal communities, as a lady from Gower recalled in the 1970s: 'Then I used to pick laver from the rocks, regularly. To help out with the mortgage on the house I used to do a regular trade with the laverbread I made. I used to sell it to local people, four pence a pound ... Oh, I love laverbread. Always have it in the house if I can.'

Laver needs to be boiled for a good 10 hours before it can be used as food. Traditionally, throughout Wales, this boiling is done with a little salt, and it continues until you have a greeny-black puree.[6] Suffice to say, to the uninitiated it is not the most appetising of foods in appearance at this point. But from here, a huge array of possibilities present themselves. Traditionally, this included making the laver into little cakes fried with oatmeal, as Camden mentions, and eating it with bacon and cockles, or using it as a delicious tangy spread on toast.

Oral memories in the 1960s from elderly people who could recall their childhoods in the 1890s give us recipes from Cardiganshire and south Pembrokeshire, and the accompanying note by Minwel Tibbott later in the 20th century: 'the most common method of cooking laverbread in the counties of South Wales was to fry it in bacon fat and serve it with bacon, usually for breakfast'.[7] This tradition carried over into the industrial coal-mining valleys, where laver and bacon was a relished Saturday morning breakfast for working class families into the late 20th century, providing a host of nutrients otherwise in short supply.[8] It was also commonly made into 'cawl lafwr' (a stew or soup) and was even served as a condiment with mutton and lamb. Bobby Freeman includes in her study of Welsh foods a recipe from a cookery book published in 1808 after the compiler, Mrs Maria Rundell, had visited Swansea. The recommendation here is that 'after roasting, Welsh mutton used to be dished with the piping hot laver "bread" mixed with Seville orange juice'.[9] More recent recipes include laverbread quiche,[10] laverbread pasta,[11] laver sauce to accompany crab,[12] or even as laver as a salad.[13] And as we shall see, the laver tradition continues today much as it has for centuries.

The largest oysters in the world

If laver today has the reputation of being a strange food only the Welsh would eat, historically the people of Wales were also well known for their liking for cockles, oysters, mussels and other shellfish (winkles, limpets). This was remarked on by numerous early tourists to Wales, often with surprise, such as the 1805 comment on the eating patterns of the cottagers of western Wales, that 'they are remarkably partial to cockles'. On the estuary of the river Conwy on the northern coast, wild mussels are still harvested today in an unbroken tradition also dating back at least to medieval times. These wild mussels are larger than the rope-grown specimens found in modern supermarkets, and are still harvested with a rake in the traditional way. But numbers are not what they once were, with a handful of men continuing a trade carried out two generations ago by ninety. The cottage industry of gathering, processing and selling the cockles that abound along parts of the southern Welsh coast is, however, one of the remarkable survival stories of Welsh food history. It stands in stark contrast to the sad story of the Welsh oyster, which is worth relaying in full and contrasting with the tale of the cockles.

Oysters were for many centuries an equally abundant source of good quality protein enjoyed in many parts of the country. Oysters from the coastal waters of the British Isles were well known and highly regarded as early as Roman times, and were exported to Rome itself, where they were considered a particular delicacy.[14] Along the coasts of Wales, the most prolific beds lay along the shores of the south and west, lapped by the warmer waters of the Gulf Stream. In particular, three parts of the coast were renowned for oyster production, all of them remarkable as places in their own right.

First the monastic gem of Caldey Island (or Ynys Bŷr in Welsh), off Tenby in Pembrokeshire, which was settled by the Celtic saint St Pŷr in the 6th century and then became a priory in 1113. Like the Scilly Isles off the coast of Cornwall, this picturesque island laced with its beaches of golden sand benefits from a distinctively mild microclimate, putting it amongst the sunniest spots anywhere in the British Isles, and hardly ever suffering from frost. This fortunate spot was also the beneficiary of an oyster bed that was known to be about 'a mile and an half in length, and a mile in breadth, lying duly to the north west of [the] island'.[15] Most of those who took advantage of this bed were town dwellers from nearby Tenby, a place that itself 'from time immemorial, is celebrated for the amazing abundance and variety of the fish tribe that haunt its shores, and the sea immediately adjacent, in allusion to which the Welsh call it Dynbegh-y-Piscoid' (literally 'Little fortress of the fish' – still the Welsh name for Tenby today).

Of all the seafood caught off Tenby and Caldey, oysters were justifiably the most famous in their day. Dr Richard Pococke of London informs his readers in 1756 that 'Tenby is famous for the largest oysters in the world; they are about 7 inches over'. More local sources seem to have agreed: the Pembrokeshire antiquarian George Owen writing in 1603 notes that the oysters from this bed were already well known for their large size in his day: '[the] greate kinde of oyster gathered at Caldey and Stackpole, which being eaten rawe, seeme too strong a meate for weake stomakes, and must be parted in two, three, or foure peeces before he may be eaten, by reason of his exceeding bignes'.[16] This was the basis not only for a local subsistence fishery but also for a booming export trade.

Two centuries after George Owen, we get a more detailed

description of the fishery and the oyster trade from these waters from the pen of traveller John Evans:

> But what this shore is most famed for is the incomparable oyster fishery … Oysters lie at all depths: … here on the shore of Caldey … the fishery, though simple, is curious, and varies according to the depth of their stations, or the means of the fishermen. Some collect them with their hands; and others with a sort of long wooden tongs, or a rake of iron spikes affixed to the end of a large pole. But these methods can only be adopted in shoal water: the most common mode of fishing, and that adopted here, is what they call dredging, from the instrument used on this occasion, a dredge … Equipped with several of these, they proceed in their boats over the oyster grounds, dislodging and collecting the oysters, often taking up the dredges as they fill, which is known by the weight, and discharging the contents into the hold of the boat. Numerous boats are occupied in this fishery, and most of the poor families here are employed in the trade, Tenby supplying the midland and western coasts of England with this article of luxury.[17]

The oysters exported from Tenby were in fact pickled oysters, a speciality of this town (and of Beaumaris in Anglesey) developed by the 1750s and possibly earlier. The fresh oyster season ran from the beginning of September till the end of April. By pickling – a food storage device that first started to be used in Britain in the 1680s[18] – the season could be extended substantially, and more profit derived from the trade. Tenby oysters were thus pickled and exported in small casks, jars, and even barrels and brought in good money to those involved in the business. The largest single destination for these oysters seems to have been the city of Bristol, where, according to contemporary accounts, some enterprising local businessmen with scant regard for the truth had taken to selling them as 'Bristol oysters', by which name they became widely known in England.[19] We get a measure of the sheer profusion of oysters in Tenby by the early 19th century from descriptions of the town that mention 'mountains of shells, the aggregate of many a century, occur in several parts of the town, forming a nuisance that would amply pay for removing'.[20]

The second area along this coastline with a noteworthy oyster fishery were the waters of Milford Haven, the largest coastal ria in the British Isles. A ria is defined as a long, narrow inlet formed by the partial submergence of a river valley and the one at Milford has been deemed strategically important for the British Crown for centuries as a safe anchorage for potentially large numbers of ships, should the need arise. Its great culinary interest however lay in oysters, which by all accounts were the most superb of all the Welsh beds:

> In various parts of Milford-haven are inexhaustible beds of oysters, of superior excellence, in such abundance, as to render them a cheap article of luxury … The oysters of Tenby, Caldey, Stackpool, &c. are remarkable for their large size, but deemed inferior in quality to those of Milford.[21]

George Owen is able to muse triumphantly on the virtues of these superior Milford oysters, 'I presume if the poet Horace had tasted of this Milford oyster, he would not have preferred the oyster of Circæi before this …', alluding to the Roman poet's discussion of the seafood delicacies enjoyed by the upper crust of ancient Rome.[22]

73

Unlike in ancient Rome, however, oysters had for centuries been a food for all parts of society, and were particularly valuable to the poor in these coastal communities who had access thereby to a cheap source of good protein. Charles Hassall, writing in 1794, explains that their value lay in 'giving employment to numbers of industrious people, at that season of the year, when their labours are at least wanted in the fields; and affording winter employment to many, who would otherwise be much distressed, for the means of supporting their families'.

This was true in other parts of Wales with access to oysters, such as Oystermouth in Gower, where 'villagers used to eat them on a regular basis and … children were fed oysters from a very early age as a cheap and easily obtainable supplement'.[23] Already in Hassall's day, however, there was a need to strike a note of warning about environmentally destructive challenges: 'But for want of some regulations for the government of the oyster fishery, there is much reason to dread [that] the breed will be totally destroyed; and that valuable source, of employment to the poor, and luxury to the opulent, be thereby cut off.'

The third of these noteworthy oyster fisheries, off Anglesey, is interesting for a different reason: it was deliberately seeded rather than occurring naturally. Oysters existed naturally in spots along the coastline of the north-west, including off Anglesey as reports from the 1740s testify.[24] But the beds off Penmon at the eastern end of the Menai straits, where the pickled oysters of Beaumaris were harvested, owed their existence to that fact that 'about a century and a half ago [i.e. in the 1680s], some beneficent person is said to have thrown about a hundred Oysters into the Menai, where they increased wonderfully, as they also do in different places by the storms driving their seeds in various directions'.[25] The oysters flourished and, by the 1740s, oysters were exported 'in plenty' from Holyhead, Caernarfon and other ports along the surrounding coastlines.[26] In stark contrast to modern conceptions of Welsh food – including by many within Wales – oysters and other seafood historically formed an important part of the diet for a great many inhabitants of the country. The diet of the common people of Anglesey, for instance, is described in a 1775 account as consisting of 'little meat, but [they] eat cheese and butter, bacon, tame and wild fowls, sea fish, oysters, crabs, lobsters, shrimps, prawns, muscles and cockles,' the word 'meat' here referring to what today we call red meat.[27]

Oysters and other shellfish were widely eaten in inland areas of Wales in season too, by virtue of the strong pull of the markets in the main market towns. Both the markets at Haverfordwest and Carmarthen were well known for the coastal produce on offer there, and they found their way by the turn of the seventeenth century to the markets of 'Cardigan, Carmarthen, Brecknock, Radnor, Monmouth, Hereford and Montgomery', covering thus a wide swathe of the country and beyond.[28] Oysters were within reach of the common people even when sold in these inland towns: a 1652 description of the foods on offer at Carmarthen market notes that the price of 100 oysters was a penny, the same as the cost of a dozen eggs or six pears at that market. The more well-to-do, who always tried to keep up with food trends in England, tended to have their oysters in elaborate sauces, or to opt for the pickled varieties. Thus for example do we read of the fare served to Richard Fenton in 1804 as he stayed with the country parson of Llanfihangel-ar-Arth, an inland area of Wales, during his tour of the country: 'Left this sublime scenery … to the snug and neat Glebe house of the Revd Mr Williams, Vicar of Llanfihangel ar arth where Mrs Williams, a very respectable Gentlewoman pressed in a strain of hospitality, rare now-a-days, to take some refreshement, and got us a veal cutlet nicely dressed, with cold Ham and Tenby pickled oysters; with the best table beer and finest ale I ever drank, but too strong.'[29]

Oysters were thus an important and widely acknowledged speciality within the Welsh diet by the turn of the 19th century, and, as industrialization got into full swing as the century progressed, demand for them only grew. Despite Hassall's warning a century before, and as so often happens when people tap into a natural stock, the beds were overexploited. Between 1850 and 1870 (a boom period for all concerned), boats at Oystermouth and Swansea were bringing in 4,000 oysters per day during the season, and the fishermen were making a healthy profit. In the year 1871, as the trade peaked and money filled pockets, 10 million oysters were landed, fetching £50,000. There were by this point over 600 men employed in the trade in this one fishery.[30] However, the seeds of decline and disaster had already been sown by this point, and when boats arrived from ports further afield to take advantage of this natural abundance, oversupply on the markets led to a collapse in price. This price collapse led to many fishermen suddenly struggling to make a living from oysters. On top of this, the beds themselves were exhausted. By 1890, those fishermen still working the oysters were bringing in catches of only 200 oysters – the population was in the process of crashing. There was further decline thereafter in the health of the fishery until in a fatal blow the oyster beds were infected by parasites in 1921.[31] Though less dramatic, similar fates befell the oyster fisheries of Milford, Anglesey and Tenby too, bringing an end not only to an important part of Welsh food culture, but also to these important parts of a delicate marine ecosystem.

There are now moves afoot to increase the oyster population and enable the development of biogenic reefs to improve water quality and enhance existing ecosystems, including efforts both in Milford Haven and at Oystermouth.[32] But taken as a whole, this is a tale of disaster – of ecological and economic mismanagement – which makes the tale of Welsh cockles all the more remarkable, not only because the two stocks are, on the surface at least, so similar to each other and were often sold in the same markets to the very same people.

Cockle country

Cockles are quite different to oysters; small, wrinkled creatures much smaller in size. They live just under the sands, and so can be picked by hand on the shore without any need for boats. Cockle beds – and other shellfish beds – are found all around the Welsh coast, from the Dee estuary on the north-eastern border all the way round to Glamorgan. We have geography to thank for this. Cockles need large areas of sand that are covered at high tide and revealed when the tide is out: Wales's many broad estuaries provide exactly the right habitat, and, thankfully, the majority of those were never much affected by heavy industry. As a result, shellfish are an important part of many coastal communities' food heritage. The ancient town of Laugharne, on the Tâf estuary in Carmarthenshire, famous for its links with Dylan Thomas, is also home to one of only two surviving medieval town corporations in the British Isles (the other is the City of London). The town's portreeve – analogous to the mayor – wears a ceremonial chain of cockle shells, with a new one added for each new portreeve to hold the post.

Symbolism aside, cockle fishing was traditionally a woman's business in Welsh communities. The beds around Carmarthen Bay were particularly important, large enough to make cockle fishing a way of life in many of the villages along the shores. The cockles the women gathered were often taken home in large containers balanced on their heads, cooked, and then taken to market the next day. John Evans described the scene at Llansteffan in 1803:

> The tide was now out, and numerous cocklers were busily engaged in their uncomfortable and ill-paid employment. These are poor females, wives and daughters of fishermen and others, that come here for the purpose of taking cockles. These fish bury themselves in the sands, and are discovered by a small bubbling, occasioned by their breathing, upon which their pursuers immediately scratch them up, put them in sacks, and carry them to the boats, which ply for this purpose between this place and Carmarthen, during high tides, at the small fare of 2d. each person. After thus toiling, and the spoil brought home, they obtain sometimes 6d. per bushel.

Later, this developed into a tradition of door to door selling. Cockles that had already been boiled and shelled would be carried around on the women's head, and were called *cocs rhython*. The uncooked cockles, still in their shells, were carried in baskets on the women's arms, were known as *cocs cregyn*, and were sold more cheaply. Between the different implements used for harvesting the cockles, the terminology and the practices around selling and preparing the cockles, an entire coastal food culture arose. Part of that culture was a particular costume that became a sort of unofficial uniform for the women; it combined practicality when out harvesting on the windswept sands, and bright colours to attract buyers at the market and on the road, as described in the Bristol Mercury in 1861: 'The milk and cockle women too make a pretty sight as they return home after disposing of their goods. They generally march along the road in bare feet, for, though they wear their shoes in the town, they generally doff them as soon as they get to the outskirts. Across their breasts they wear a small red handkerchief, and their dresses reach only to the knee.'[33]

This dress was considered exotic and romantic by Victorian travellers, who got many a cockle-woman to pose for paintings and later for photographs. These were popular enough to contribute to the partly artificial notion of Welsh national dress, with shawl and flannel apron and distinctive, tall hats for the women:

> The cockle women look very picturesque in their short gowns of red and black flannel, which are turned up in front and pinned close under the waist at the back. These gowns display neat, short petticoats of Welsh flannel. Small turnover shawls are worn over the shoulders, and flannel aprons protect the dress in front. On their heads they wear small Welsh hats, suitable for bearing the weight of the cockle pails … A thick pad, known as a 'dorch', protects both the hat and the head from the pail.[34]

It was then no exaggeration to call certain coastal parts of Wales cockle-country; even the paths and garden walls in many of these villages were decorated with discarded cockle shells. Most importantly of all, there were numerous recipes associated with them. One common dish involved boiling the cockles in a reasonable quantity of milk, adding chives or parsley and some salt. Flour was then blended with cold milk and this would be poured gradually into the boiling mixture. This thick cockle sauce was then served with *bara menyn*. There were also several variations on cockle pies, with shortcrust pastry, chives and then either cheese or bacon, all cooked in an oven. Yet another tradition developed around the large cockle beds of the Dwyryd estuary in north-west Wales from Cricieth along the coast to Penrhyndeudraeth, as represented by the raunchy ditty sung by the women who sold the dish:

> Cocos a wya
> Bara ceirch tena
> Merched y Penrhyn
> Yn ysgwyd u tina!

> Cockles and eggs,
> Thin oatbread sliced
> The Penrhyn girls' butts
> All lookin' nice

This was Welsh street food, *avant l'heure*. Eggs and cockles fried together in bacon fat with a pinch of salt and pepper. Some people added strips of bacon too. This was then served hot between slices of oatbread or barley bread. It was considered a delicacy in the area and was widely available to buy in season, either on the street or at the markets along the coast between Pwllheli and Harlech.

Penclawdd

A few companies continue to harvest both cockles and laver commercially in southern Wales today. One of these, that has continued an age-long tradition of harvesting seafood in the Loughor estuary, the old cockle heartland, is Selwyn's.

'Selwyn was my dad,' explains Brian, the current owner of the business, based in the estuary village of Penclawdd, 'and he started paying tax on his cockle business in 1950. But that's not when my family's involvement in this trade started.' Penclawdd has long been synonymous with shellfish. Different families traditionally harvested different things from the estuary, in an unwritten agree-ment between them. But they were all united in being known as the people who would 'go out the sands'.

The sands is an apt term for the broad, windswept Loughor estuary that stretches north of Gower to where the whale-back Carmarthenshire hills drop down to the sea. It is an area five miles wide at its widest point, and almost ten miles long, where sand, sea and salt-marsh merge imperceptibly, and where the border between land and sea shifts incessantly back and forth. One moment, gentle blue waves lap the shore at Penclawdd, and the sun sparkles all the way across the foam to Llanelli on the other side. A couple of hours later and sheep are grazing a mile or two out, and beyond that golden sand beds roll away to the low channel of the Loughor river. But this landscape, in all its shifting change, has fed people for thousands of years.

Selwyn's father was a miner, but he would help his mother in gathering flatfish (bass and others) and shellfish (both mussels and cockles) from the estuary. In a stroke of misfortune with its own silver lining, Selwyn was hit by a van driven by a US soldier who was stationed near Penclawdd during the Second World War. The soldier who hit him was killed not long after in the fighting, but the US government paid Selwyn compensation for the injury. With that money Selwyn bought a truck that enabled him to go and sell cock-les in the larger markets of Swansea and then Merthyr. He returned from his first trip with a profit and his uncle said, 'Selwyn, where have you been to have this money?' Selwyn explained his idea. 'Go again', said his uncle, and that was the beginning of Selwyn's as a cockle business in the modern sense, with a market across southern Wales and eventually beyond.

'Of course, back in the day', Brian muses, 'the cockles and the laver and all that were just something that had always been about' in those parts of Wales. Everybody round on the coasts would be harvesting laver in the winter. In an era when a quarter of a million men worked in the coal mines of the valleys, there was great demand for laver to combat the high incidence of anaemia among the male population from the long periods spent underground. It was perceived – rightly – to be a particularly nutritious foodstuff, and was given to children 'for their health'. Brian laughs: 'Of course, it isn't an attractive looking food, the laver! But because they all grew up on it, they ate it. On bread with butter they ate it.'

But cockles were the mainstay of the business down the decades. Selwyn would take his van around the towns and cities of southern Wales, ringing his heavy hand bell as he drove slowly down the street. Relationships were built as people became regular customers. In time, the fleet grew to six vans that covered the whole of southern Wales, with Brian driving one down to Cardiff for many years. 'People know me. I've stopped that now, though my son-in-law is still doing a little of the van business. But the people I used to go to, a lot of them now come up here to fetch the cockles and the seafood for themselves.'

This rings a poignant bell for me, evoking memories of growing up in a terraced house in inner-city Cardiff in the 1990s. I suddenly have a vague recollection of fish vans on our street when I was young, and seeing neighbours buying cockles. I ask my Mam, and sure enough, the vans came to our neighbourhood, even ringing the old bell. We didn't buy the cockles from the van, but we would sometimes have some as a snack when shopping on Clifton Street, the local shopping street that in those days retained butchers, bakers, fishmongers, greengrocers, cobblers, locksmiths and of course a Blockbuster video rental shop. Served in throwaway polystyrene cups with a wooden fork, and often sprinkled with malt vinegar, this was a moreish snack, no less exciting and certainly no more exotic to my brother and me than a bag of crisps. Sometimes it was the latter, sometimes the cockles – except that by the end, they were marketed as 'seafood cocktail'.

It was in the 1980s that seaweed became part of Selwyn's business, with the decline of the old Gower families. 'Laver was Bishopston with the Roaches in the old days, see,' says Brian, 'and in Penclawdd here it was the Roberts. They made it, we sold it.' But then, in the 1980s, the seaweed started going short, and a lot of the other families gradually stopped making it. So Selwyn started going and making his own. But the tidal mudflats and salt marshes of the Loughor on the north side of Gower were never laver territory. The seaweed had always come from the wind-marked beaches on the southern coast of Gower, or from further west in Pembrokeshire – around the St Davids headland, down in Castlemartin and along Carmarthen Bay westwards from Laugharne. Selwyn would occasionally go out west in a van himself during the laver season, but mostly he'd find the people who were already there, gathering, and buy the laver from them. Those relationships have continued to this day, with local foragers supplying the company with most of its laver from Pembrokeshire.

Things changed in the early 2000s. The market for seafood had declined in Wales, just as the number of suppliers was also dwindling. Dutch companies established themselves in the Thames estuary cockle fishery, and, over time, companies from both the Netherlands and Spain tried to buy out Selwyn's too. 'I refused to sell,' says Brian simply, 'I done this all my life. I love going out there on the sands. I used to go out with a horse when I was young. I been out there this morning – do you think I don't have enough to do in this office?' he says with an expansive gesture. 'But I love the work too much.'

They decided to look to grow their own market, and create one if need be. Dried laver products were a part of that – creating dried seaweed squares, flavoured with salt and vinegar, or chilli. Sea-crisps, if you like, that are now sold in delis and upmarket supermarkets throughout Wales. But for the cockles, the Spanish market was indispensable. They came to an agreement with Dani, a family-owned seafood company from Barcelona that supplies a large Spanish supermarket chain: '90% of all the cockles we harvest go there, 24 tonnes at a time get transported live to Galicia! The market here is small now for the amount we have here. I know people used to eat them all the time, but it isn't like that no more.'

The biggest threat to the fishery came with the wreck of the Sea Empress off the Pembrokeshire coast in 1989. Brian had just got a loan to expand the factory in Penclawdd the very day the news came through. The forecast was unambiguous – the wind and tide would carry the oil slick across Carmarthen Bay that very night, and straight up the Loughor estuary. Any shellfish that survived would with absolute certainty be classed unfit to eat: 'I thought that would be the end of us. I remember thinking we are going to have to convert this to a Welshcake factory or something.' But the wind direction changed, and the oil was carried away off south. None came up the estuary, and when Brian went out the next morning, there lay the beds as they always had; just the matt-brown sand and seabirds circling overhead.

As of 2019, the stocks remain abundant, and generally in good health: 200 tonnes of cockles a day could be harvested in Carmarthen Bay on the shores off Kidwelly, Ferryside and Laugharne during the season between May and Christmas. In recent years, however, stocks seem to have died off early in July, during the week of the Royal Welsh Show. 'We don't know why that is – the universities at Aber and Bangor are looking into it. But I do think there's not enough harvesting going on like there used to be. We need to take the pressure off the beds by thinning the cockles out. Today we had 20 or 25 people out on the sands. But back in 2005, at the height of the season, there might have been a thousand people out there picking during the daylight hours. It's because we're the only ones left now – and most of our people are over 55 years old, I'd say.'

They are still gathering by hand, Brian tells me, though how long that will continue he doesn't know. It's slowly becoming uneconomical because of the labour costs: 'Our people will go out there with a rake and a bucket, and we're looking at harvesting 6 tonnes each tide. They rake the sand, pick the cockles, shake them about with the sieve and then in the bucket they go.' By harvesting in the traditional way and riddling by hand, gatherers can sort out cockles that are below the minimum landing size and return them immediately to the sands. The returned cockles can re-burrow and breed, thus contributing to the sustainability of the stocks. 'We then cook on site the cockles we don't export within two hours. Those cooked cockles we sell directly to restaurants or they go places like Swansea market. But most of them are gone in the lorries, off to Spain and so on.'

The fishery, although only a few square miles in size, is internationally significant. In some years, its production has almost equalled that of all other cockle fisheries in Britain put together, despite the fact that this is the only major cockle fishery in the UK that continues to use the ancient rake and sieve methods. Dredging and mechanical harvesting using tractors were allowed on the Dee estuary and in Morecambe Bay from the 1970s, but we have a licensing system to thank for their refusal on the Penclawdd beds. This system permits a limited number of licences only, 55 a year or so, issued for the hand-raking of cockles only. No night collection is allowed, and there is a maximum quota per person per day. As a result, it is widely acknowledged to be the most ecologically sustainable cockle fishery in the UK.[35] The licensing system has also kept the business local, meaning that situations that have arisen elsewhere in the UK, with migrant workers employed to work treacherous sands leading in some cases to tragic deaths, have been avoided.[36]

It's hard not to admire the hard graft that Brian, like his father before him, has put in to working on an old cottage-economy livelihood and making it profitable in the rapidly changing world of the last sixty years. And what becomes abundantly clear from talking to him, and learning about the state of the remaining laver and shellfish businesses, is that these are precarious markets, clinging on. Most guidebooks and tourist articles on Wales talk about the cockle territory between Swansea and Llanelli, and laver is often mentioned as a local delicacy. But those 'top ten flavours of Wales' or 'local specialities' articles hide the realities on the ground, which is that, despite the roots and the unbroken traditions, it is adaptation to national or international economic forces that is the order of the day – thus far at least. It would take the growth of a new indigenous market for cockles, mussels and laver to change that.

So despite the success story that cockles represent, at least in comparison with oysters, my conversation with Brian ends on a melancholic note. Like many of the native food traditions, the cockle harvest at Penclawdd was traditionally carried out by women. 'It was all the women of the village that did it,' as Brian explains, 'but that's gone now. We're not the only ones left in this estuary – not quite – but we are the only ones now that do the great beds in Carmarthen Bay, keeping them going.'

Too far for you to see
The fluke and the foot-rot and the fat maggot
Gnawing the skin from the small bones,
The sheep are grazing at Bwlch-y-Fedwen,
Arranged romantically in the usual manner
On a bleak background of bald stone.

R. S. Thomas, mid-20th century

Pam, Arglwydd, y gwnaethost Gwm Pennant mor dlws,
A bywyd hen fugail mor fyr?

Why, Lord, did you make Cwm Pennant so beautiful
And the life of this old shepherd so short?

Eifion Wyn, late 19th century

4

OEN AC EIDION / LAMB AND BEEF

The hills and mountains of Wales throng today with seasonal visitors. Imagine the scene on Snowdon, highest peak in the British Isles south of the Scottish Highlands, on a balmy Saturday in July. Above and below the tourist-filled paths lies the unchanging landscape. Sheep dot the crags and rocks, and ravens circle over-head. The valley-bottoms are farmed still, with infields arranged neatly around the old stone farmhouses. The sheep, of course, belong to these farms, sheep-farming being synonymous with much of the Welsh countryside. The fate of these farming families and their way of life often makes the news: one day, they are respon-sible for climate change. Another day, they are a relic of a bygone age, their existence underwritten by unsustainable subsidies paid for from the public purse. The next time they are mentioned, it's in connection with the need to rewild these mountain areas, now widely considered sheep-wrecked by environmental campaigners. But regardless of the opinion, one thing seems clear to everyone: these hills have always been full of sheep.

Sheep define much of the Welsh landscape, and many people's image of Welsh farming and food. Welsh lamb has become a mainstay of the agricultural sector, and is widely recognized to be of high quality, fetching premium prices compared to lamb produced in other parts of the British Isles or indeed the world. This has to do with the combination of farming methods, landscapes, climate and breeds, with sheep raised everywhere from the high peaks of Snowdonia down to gentler hills and the saltmarshes of the coast.

The defining Welsh ingredient today has thus indisputably become lamb, and it is now often married with the most iconic of Welsh dishes, *cawl*; the native meat-based broth with leek and root vegetables. The two components are often brought together to form the quintessence of Welsh food, fulfilling both foreign and native stereotypes of the country's cuisine: *cawl cig oen* or 'lamb cawl'. We will follow the story of cawl in the final chapter, but despite lamb's ubiquity as a core ingredient in modern variations on cawl, historically dishes of 'lamb cawl' would have been hard to find in Wales. Today though you can find lamb cawl (called *lobsgows* in northern Wales) – as a lamb stew made with leeks, potatoes and other root vegetables such as carrots, swedes and parsnips served with crusty bread and cheese – throughout the country, from cafés in Cardiff to posh rural gastropubs in the Vale of Clwyd and on kitchen tables and at St David's Day potluck meals throughout the country. The enduring popularity of cawl has undoubtedly been a help to lamb's prospects, but its status as Wales's quintessential food product today also has much to do with the climate, topography and location of the country. With abundant rainfall, large areas of upland unsuitable under conventional 20th century agriculture for much else, and a strong pastoral tradition, the stage was set for lamb to become indissolubly associated with the country once the final ingredient – fashion – had played its part.

There are worse culinary fates than to have lamb represent your national cuisine; according to Hugh Fearnley-Whittingstall lamb is the most naturally succulent of all the meats, able to reach 'pretty astronomical levels of savoury deliciousness', partly due to the thymol it contains, a natural flavour-creating constituent also found in thyme.[1] It is naturally free-range, usually pasture-fed, and rich in iron, vitamin B12 and high-quality proteins. And by the latter half of the 20th century, Welsh lamb was widely acknowledged to be of high quality, with European PGI[2] status awarded in 2003. Lamb's fat content is around 20%, found in two forms – phospholipids and triglyceride – and this fatty acid mix gives it a more complex flavour than beef, particularly when grass-fed. When put in a stew with leeks, carrots, potatoes and swedes, which is then cooked slowly on a low heat, as in cawl, the lamb fat lends the whole a delicate, mildly sweet flavour. I have had bowls of cawl before (made by my mother, of course) where I have wondered whether apple juice, or slices of pear had been added, such was the fruity sweetness. Shock and horror were the response to the mere suggestion: the sweetness all comes from the succulent young lamb. At its best, a marriage made in culinary heaven.

We get a detailed description of what went into a normal family's cawl in the early 19th century from the English traveller, Heath Malkin, and on close investigation lamb seems not to be as indissolubly linked to cawl as we might have expected: 'Broths made from all sorts of meat are much used; in which large quantities of potherbs and other vegetables form a principal ingredient; abundance of leeks, onions, shalots, parsley, savoury, pennyroyal, marjoram, thyme, cresses, beets, lettuces, spinage, and other productions of the garden. Herb broth, as it is called, is much used by the common people ... and [they] take it with bread.' Malkin's reference here to 'all sorts of meat' clearly broadens the scope of the recipe and would have alluded to beef, pork and mutton, depending on circumstances and season.

Many traditional recipes for cawl, including numerous family recipes still in use today, dictate the use of beef rather than lamb, often accompanied with bacon. And in reality, beef has at least as strong a claim to the top rung of the Welsh meat pedestal as does lamb (or, as we shall see, mutton). There is a culturally significant tradition of cattle rearing in Wales, with the hardy Welsh black, which does well on rough grazing, considered by the food critic Mark Price to be the best beef breed available today, beating both the better-known Hereford and Angus: 'It presents a well-conformed eye muscle and just the right level of fat to allow a nice layer on the back (to protect during ageing) as well as the perfect amount of marbling in the muscle.'[3] Despite this, it was never as widely consumed by the Welsh as were mutton or pork. This is strongly related to the fact that beef was for centuries of greater importance economically, and the story of beef production as a commodity for the export market, and the drovers at the centre of that story, forms a fascinating counterpoint to the more domestically oriented rearing of sheep and goats in the country which led eventually to the rise of lamb.

Drovers

Cattle were the principal store of wealth in early Welsh society, as was also true in medieval Irish and Scottish society. They had more than a purely economic function, and were viewed as having symbolic and even supernatural importance. This is reflected in Irish mythology, with the cattle-raid of Cooley featuring as the centre-piece of one of Irish literature's most influential pieces. The Welsh *Mabinogi* does not feature cattle quite as heavily (wild boar, horses and fields of wheat are more prominent), but other early Welsh texts confirm the culture's interest in cattle:

> Three Principal Cows of the Island of Britain:
> Speckled, cow of Maelgwn Gwynedd,
> and Grey-Skin, cow of the sons of Eliffer of the
> Great Warband,
> and Cornillo, cow of Llawfrodedd the Bearded.[4]

This is one of the ancient 'Triads of the Island of Britain' (lists of important things or people in poetic form) and already at this early date, cattle are associated strongly with aristocratic figures. This tendency is taken further in the 10th century laws of King Hywel Dda, the body of native Welsh law. This put a greater emphasis on compensation than on punishment, and sets the price for numerous infringements both in monetary terms and in terms of the cost in cattle.

But the real impetus for the commodification of the Welsh cow came not from within Welsh society, but from neighbouring England. The old French moniker for the English – *les rosbifs* – from 'roast beef', has more than a little basis in reality. Old John Bull's fondness for roast beef started early. By the time of Elizabeth's reign in the 16th century, the English love affair with meat, and with beef in particular, was already drawing comment from foreigners visiting the country.[5] This was more a reflection of those who were more or less comfortably off than of the diet of either urban or rural poor; but it made an impression. Power in England – and later in

Britain – had long been concentrated in and around London, and as a result, wealthy Londoners' taste for beef had to be assuaged, even if the surrounding countryside wasn't particularly well suited to doing so. Rainfall and climate are in no small part responsible for this: the dominant westerly winds in the British Isles keep the western parts well-watered, and generally give a longer growing season for grass. The east, where London is situated, suffers from more extreme drought in summer, and from freezing temperatures in winter – all of which makes it less congenial for cattle-rearing at a sufficient scale to satisfy the local appetite for beef. (It's interesting to note in passing that this made the upper classes' desire for beef unsustainable, in that it surpassed the ecological carrying capacity of the city's hinterland. As a result, the ecological potential of regions further away were drawn upon: a process that happens today on a global scale.)

As a result, from the 14th century, and perhaps earlier, cattle were driven from Welsh pastures to supply the London court with its beef. By the time English roast beef was being commented upon by foreigners, a good deal of that same beef had started its life on the Welsh hills and mountains. After the Acts of Union in 1536, this burgeoning trade presented Welsh nobles and other landowners with a golden opportunity to corner a growing market, and to use the comparative economic advantages at their disposal – cheaper land, plentiful cattle, cheap labour – to make good money in the wealthier markets of England's cities and larger towns.

By the time the English civil war was ravaging both countries in the 1640s, Bishop John Williams of Conwy was able to make a petition to the Crown that the warring armies provide the drovers with safe passage because they were 'Wales's Spanish Fleet, providing us with what little gold and silver we have'.[6] The petition was granted, and from 1645 drovers were given special dispensation for free passage along the routes they used, which by this point had become a web of roads crossing Wales and central England, always converging on the metropolis that was London.

The drovers themselves became in some ways a class apart: coming as they did from upland areas of Wales, sometimes far from outside influences, they became the conduit for new ideas, fashions and news. They combined the glamour of the cosmopolitan with the figure of the road-weary traveller, familiar with the high mountain passes and the lonely hill roads. Around them, entire ways of life and regional economies were built. Young women would travel with the drovers and their cattle to London to look for seasonal work, giving rise to numerous references to Welsh women selling vegetables and fruit in London markets.[7] Pubs and inns in several parts of England bore inscriptions in Welsh, advertising 'gwair tymherus, porfa flasus, cwrw da, gwâl gysurus': hay, grazing, beer and a bed! The corgi breed of Welsh dog (cor-gi = dwarf dog), bred for herding livestock, owes its familiarity in England to its use by drovers. The drovers developed a distinctive unofficial uniform, with wide-brimmed hats, a particular type of staff and drinking implements. And wide roads leading from Welsh towns across mountains and then the English lowlands all developed thanks to the drovers in a period well before the post-routes were established.

The cattle were all breeds native to Wales, from Anglesey down to Pembrokeshire. They varied in colour – some black, others red, grey, white, brown, speckled or striped. The lowland breeds were significantly larger in size than their hardy mountain cousins. Large Anglesey cattle were used as oxen in Sussex in the 1830s, and were commonly bought for a few years of work before being sold to the London market for beef. But the mainstay of the droving economy relied on what the English called 'Welsh runts'. These were the mountain cattle, small and tough, that could cope with the weeks of travel from Snowdonia or the hills of Ceredigion to the summer pastures near London. There they feasted on grass, and quickly put on weight for slaughter.[8]

Sometimes, particularly in the early years of the trade, drovers worked in the service of local nobility. But as time went on, and droving became a trade in its own right, the drovers became independent operators and they would buy cattle (often on credit) from farmers or dealers. The majority of their cattle were purchased at local fairs, many of which took place on a vast scale. When the Rev. Evans visited Cilgerran Fair near Cardigan in 1804, he noted that all the fields within three miles of the village were full of cattle, and that 'the number of cattle, though this was considered a small fair, we were informed exceeded 20,000'.[9]

The size of the drovers' trade in cattle grew over the centuries, until it reached a crescendo in the 19th century shortly before the arrival of the railways. By the early 19th century, the extent of the demand for Welsh cattle can be seen in the fact that scarcely any account books from the English midlands during this period do not refer to the purchase of Welsh cattle at some time of the year.[10] In 1750 a total of 70,000 cattle were sold at London's Smithfield market; by 1830 that number had reached 160,000.[11] The size of the droves coming from Wales reflected this enormous number. The agricultural commentator William Cobbett reported meeting 2,000 cattle being driven across the Cotswolds en route from Pembrokeshire to cattle fairs in Sussex.

The sights, sounds and smells of this trade must have been overwhelming at times, judging from contemporary accounts. A group of drovers, surrounded by yapping dogs, sticks in the air, swearing and shouting 'ai ai ai ai!' Cattle – an enormous animal mass of them – trundling past. Flies, grunts, sweat. As the *Farmers' Magazine* put it in the 1850s, 'imagine hundreds of bullocks and an immense forest of horns, propelled hurriedly towards you amid the hideous and uproarious shouting of a set of semi-barbarous drovers who value a restive bullock far beyond the life of a human being, driving their mad and noisy herds over every person they meet … lots of un-English speaking Welshmen!' Another contemporary commentator put it wryly when describing the scene as the Welsh drovers descended on the London cattle fairs, 'a wilder or more noisy scene it is difficult to conceive'.[12]

As well as being a significant part of the economy of both Wales and England for centuries, the trade also shaped both countries' cuisines in different ways. English beef-eating, enabled by this trade, formed an important part of English views of their culture. And the ready market for cattle provided a good source of income for farmers, dealers, craftsmen (e.g. blacksmiths) and drovers in many parts of Wales. But, within Wales, it also led to a general shortage of beef, and seems to have contributed to the higher consumption of other meats – goat, mutton, bacon – instead. Aristocratic English visitors to the country, aware that Wales was the source of much of their beef, remarked with surprise on the difficulty of finding any when visiting the country itself. They were informed by locals that beef was in short supply precisely because all the cattle had been bought for the English markets – but some could be obtained by sending to England.[13]

Droving also led to the establishment of fairs, and in turn, of banks. It is no exaggeration to say that the drovers' cattle trade was one of the early streams of capitalism, with much of the trade dependent on letters of credit. The time lag between buying cattle in, say, Carmarthenshire, and returning from a successful sale in London with money in hand was not insignificant – measured in months, not weeks. The eventual price obtained for the cattle could vary, and the route both to and fro could lead to mishap in the form of illness, drowning, thieves. Credit was thus developed as an essential way of underwriting the financial risk involved in trade at this scale. The high levels of risk also led to the issuing of bank-notes – virtually unknown in Wales before this time – and created a group of people with networks throughout the country familiar with financial transactions of this nature. Both in London and in Wales this financial activity contributed significantly to the development of modern banking. The Welsh banks had evocative names – Banc y Ddafad Ddu (The Black Sheep Bank) in Aberystwyth, for instance, or Banc yr Eidion Du (The Black Ox Bank) in Llandovery.[14] But the London legacy was ultimately more influential, and can still be seen in the name of the London stock exchange – stock denoting originally live-stock.

Droving as a practice was ultimately rendered unprofitable and thus redundant by the arrival and proliferation of the railways. Welsh industry had a part to play here: coal, slate, copper, iron were all produced on a large scale in Wales, and fuelled much of the British empire's colonial expansion. As a result, railways penetrated most parts of the country comparatively quickly (certainly when compared to most northern European countries), and the cattle could be loaded onto trucks and taken to market much more quickly than any droving on foot or horseback. The last Welsh drovers were in fact sheep drovers, who would walk their flocks to livestock markets within Wales, a practice ultimately also brought to an end by another new method of transport, the lorry.

And so outside perceptions of Welsh meat consumption, and

the apparent love for sheep, pigs and goat, was more than a mere question of taste – and it was certainly not driven by an inability to breed and raise good beef cattle in Wales. But with the vast majority of the beef being raised exported into England for many centuries, meat-eating traditions in Wales had to develop in different directions. One element of this was that pigs became ubiquitous, with salted pork, ham and bacon providing a dietary lifeline through long, hard winters for poor cottagers across the country – judging by outsiders' comments, to an even greater extent than was true in other parts of northern Europe. Different cuts of pork later formed the basis for faggots, the fast-food delicacy of industrial southern Wales. But one meat that would hardly ever have been used in Welsh cawl before the 20th century was lamb, as sheep were simply too valuable to be killed in their youth. For today's 'Welsh lamb', we need to look at yesterday's 'Welsh mutton'.

Mutton

Sheep farming in Wales has its origins in pre-Roman times. Sheep and goats were kept in upland parts of the country where climate and soil conditions made the growing of grains or other crops nigh on impossible, and where cattle wouldn't thrive either. By medieval times, older dark-fleeced types had been interbred with white sheep imported by the Romans to produce the ancestors of today's Welsh-mountain sheep. The primary economic significance of sheep in this period didn't lie in meat or dairy produce, but in their fleeces. Wool was exported in ever greater volumes through the Middle Ages, accounting for two-thirds of Welsh exports by 1660. But unlike cattle, wool could be exported while the milk and meat were used at home. There is, then, some truth in the stereotype: sheep became an economic mainstay, and an entire culture and way of life took shape around sheep herding, with its own practices and laws (such as grazing rights).

At the centre of this was the practice of transhumance, with flocks of sheep and families of shepherds moving seasonally up onto the higher pastures, the *ffridd* in summer, and down to the valley bottoms and lowland farms for the winter. These higher pastures burst into life with the return of warmth in May and June, and, as a liminal zone between the moorland and bog often found on the hilltops and the sheltered valley bottoms, the rich growth of the flowers, grasses and shrubs provided nurturing grazing and browsing for the sheep and lambs, which was stored in their bodies as fat for the lean winters. Unsurprisingly, mutton became an important and recognized part of the Welsh diet. In 1698, one Celia Fiennes, an early English tourist to Wales, describes the diet of the people of Holywell, in the north-east: 'their meate is very small here, mutton is noe bigger than lamb, what of it there is was sweete.'[15] A little over a century and a half later, the most celebrated travel book on Wales was written by the Englishman George Borrow. In it he describes one of his first meals on his tramp around the country, where mutton is served from the hills south of the inn in Llangollen:

> For dinner we had salmon and leg of mutton; the salmon from the Dee, the leg from the neighbouring Berwyn … as for the leg of mutton it is truly wonderful; nothing so good have I ever tasted in the shape of a leg of mutton. The leg of mutton of Wales beats the leg of mutton of any other country, and I had never tasted a Welsh leg of mutton before. Certainly I shall never forget the first Welsh leg of mutton which I tasted, rich but delicate, replete with juices derived from the aromatic herbs of the noble Berwyn, cooked to a turn and weighing just four pounds

The quality of Welsh mutton was widely acknowledged both inside and outside the country. Writing for a domestic audience, David Thomas praises Meirionydd, in the mountainous north-west, for the excellence of its mutton in his poetic tour of the counties in 1750; '[yma] mae'r defaid cigog brafa yng Nghymru' / 'here are found the best meat-sheep in the country'. The London physician Thomas Moufet writing during the reign of Elizabeth I notes that in contrast to the 'rank' Somerset and Lincolnshire mutton available in London, Welsh mutton, was much more 'pleasant in eating'. Similarly, Dorothy Hartley, the English food-writer of the early 20th century wrote, 'now the small Welsh mutton is acceptedly the best. The herds are free-ranging, and on most of the hills there is an abundance of wild thyme, the spicy herb which gives Welsh mutton its characteristic flavour. The joints are very small, so that a hindquarter is cut quite usually as a leg ...'.[16]

Today, sheep remain easily the largest single component of Welsh agriculture. In 2017 the number of sheep passed the 10 million mark, nearly a third of the total for the whole of the UK. And despite a degree of homogenization, most of those sheep are native breeds, with many rare breeds surviving on farms in different parts of the country. They all carry evocative names: the Badgerface Welsh Mountain Sheep, the Black Welsh mountain, the Hill Radnor, the Llanwenog, the Brecknock Hill, the Kerry Hill, the Llandovery, the Whiteface Hill, the Lleyn, the South Wales mountain, the Welsh Hill speckled, the Welsh mountain, the Beulah and the rare Balwen. Almost all of these names are geographical in origin, tying the breed to a patch of hill country where it originated, and the conditions to which it would have adapted. And each has its own particular character and strengths – some hardier, some better for wool, others better for milk. There is something similar to the concept of *terroir* in this – except that it is a mammalian terroir on four legs, with the sheep farmer playing the role of the vigneron.

Despite its prominence and long history, sheep farming's value to Wales today lies more in its role in sustaining rural and upland communities, than in the economic returns it brings. As of 2019 the average subsidy for a Welsh upland sheep farm was £23,000 – barely enough to keep body and soul together, let alone raise a family or invest in the farm itself.[17] For many, it is a tough physical life, with long days, scant comfort and no prospects. With changes to subsidy regimes, and a strong imperative to plant many more trees in upland parts to alleviate flood risks downstream in a changing climate, it's hard not to see the number of sheep and sheep farms throughout the country declining over the years ahead. But it's equally hard to imagine the long tradition disappearing. Suggestions of rewilding and ecosystem restoration in the hills of mid-Wales have been met with rancour and no small degree of animosity from farming communities, and indeed from wider parts of the Welsh public sphere. A rapprochement between the two camps, with an acknowledgement of the key role that grazers play in a grassland ecosystem, is surely possible.

Still, despite the historic praise for mutton, only a vanishingly small proportion of Welsh sheep are raised for mutton today. Lamb has almost entirely displaced its close relation, and the reason is almost entirely to do with fashion. Slaughtering sheep when still lambs was originally a form of conspicuous consumption; a choice that a privileged few could afford to make for the sake of more tender meat. But with the economic growth of the 20th century, food markets becoming increasingly global and the decline of the wool industry, the agricultural logic of not slaughtering young lost much of its salience. As Wales grew wealthier through the course of the 20th century, fashions changed, and lamb came to be favoured – initially as a mark of people's new-found wealth. Mutton became evermore associated with the older generations, poverty and poor taste – and of course, it is tougher meat that takes longer to cook, even if it has its own slightly gamey strengths. Where pre-First World War mothers had used mutton in a dish, their daughters substituted lamb.

Weobley Castle

Not all sheep-farming in Wales is done on the wet hills that form the backbone of the country, however. Some of Wales's most prized lamb is produced on the country's shores – and here, mutton is staging a slow comeback. Weobley Castle (pronounced 'Web-lee') stands proud on a promontory in the north-western corner of Gower, dominating an estuarine landscape that rises to whale-back hills on both sides. Built by the Norman de la Bere family between 1304 and 1327 as a defensive manor-house, the castle has seen untold generations of sheep graze the windswept Llanrhidian salt-marshes that stretch out below.

'It is special out there on the marsh', Will, one of the Pritchard sons now farming here, tells me, 'you have all this space and quiet just to you and the sheep, going on for miles and miles. You never see anyone there, apart from very rarely there might be a cockle-picker out on the sands.' Will and his brother Dan are the third generation of Pritchards to farm at Weobley Castle alongside their father, Rowland, with 1,300 sheep in their care living on the marsh. Like almost all Welsh sheep farms, whether upland or lowland, this is a family farm, operating on a small scale and deeply rooted in their community and on their land.

Their day starts early, letting the four sheepdogs out for a run around 6 a.m. Then it's time to check the tides, the masters of life on this farm. High tide, twice a day, normally sees half the marsh underwater. But with a high spring tide, or a high September tide, the whole marsh will go under. 'Obviously when that happens, we need to bring the sheep fully off the marsh. They come up to the fields around the house, and then we let them back out onto the marsh when the tide's gone down. But really, apart from lambing they will spend pretty much the whole year out on the marsh'. The Pritchards need to know this land, just as a mountain farmer needs to know the hillsides. Familiarity with the climate, and the micro-climates of the terrain; the pitfalls and dangers are all an essential part of the knowledge needed to produce good food from this environment.

On a day like today with a high tide just before midnight and then again at midday, Rowland and Dan go down mid-morning, two hours or so before high tide. The dogs will run next to their quads down the causeway track that runs north from the castle out onto the marsh. The sheep are spread all over this part of the marsh, which they share with sheep from two neighbouring farms with ancient grazing rights to the salt-marshes. The marsh extends to over 4,000 acres in total. The furthest sheep might be a good two miles out from solid land, where the marsh gives way to sands. But the sheep don't mind at all; these are hardy sheep, Welsh hill mules crossed with Suffolk rams. 'Yes, they're nimble. They avoid the pills [a Gower word for the sinuous inlets that fill first with the incoming tide, and criss-cross the marsh like veins], no problem. They know what to do, they move themselves. They're clever, these sheep,' says Will, before laughing wryly, 'well ... they are still sheep!'

The saltmarshes are a good environment for sheep. The salt-water that permeates their environment hinders the development of some common diseases, like footrot. The fact that different flocks mingle does create a risk of scab or other diseases spreading quickly, but as Will explains, 'We do joined-up treatment with our neighbours for that reason, so that all the flocks on the marsh get what they're due at the same time.'

But beyond this, the sheep thrive on the rich, varied diet the marsh-plants offer them. Samphire, sorrel, sea lavender and thrift all grow in abundance on the briny marshland and form a highly nutritious diet for the sheep. The vegetation is unique, living as it does in a liminal zone that is half-sea, half-land. Even the grass species are quite different to those found up on dry land, as the tale of the next marsh over to the west, Cwm Ivy, puts in sharp focus.

Cwm Ivy marsh is a smaller parcel of land that was reclaimed from the sea to be used as farmland in the 17th century. For centuries, a sea wall held back the tides, meaning Cwm Ivy became a low-lying freshwater marsh, with fields of pastures separated by mixed hedges of tree-species typical to the area – hawthorns, alder, hazel and some planted pines. But the heavy rains of winter 2013 put pressure on the sea wall, and the landowners, the National Trust, had recently decided because of climate change that it simply wasn't viable to maintain sea walls and dykes of this sort all along the coast of Britain.[18] Abandoned to the elements, the sea wall was breached that winter, with the summer storms of August 2014 washing away so many sections that the walls quickly became redundant.

Over the next few months, as the sea washed over the marsh, the vegetation changed dramatically. Within days, the farmland grasses had died back and the trees were dropping leaves. By the following spring, what was left of the trees had become dead wood. The colours of the marsh changed, from the bright greens of the grasses that had formerly dominated the ecosystem to the much darker matt green of the salt-resistant grasses that were replacing them. And by the spring of 2015, saltmarsh plants were starting to appear – different samphires, sea blight, thrift and sea spurrey. Within two years, Cwm Ivy was already a fully functioning salt marsh, with the vegetation supporting a vibrant insect life, which in turn brought back a greater variety of coastal birds and even ospreys.

The Welsh coastline as a whole is rich in salt-marshes, long known in Welsh as *morfa*: Morfa Harlech, Morfa Rhuddlan, Morfa Cydweli. They span the length of the Welsh coast, alternating with the high sea-cliffs and sandy coves that otherwise form the coastline. But although less dramatic than cliffs and coves, they are more important ecologically: salt-marshes are one of the most biologically productive habitats on earth, rivalling tropical rainforests. The low-lying estuaries and bays of the North Atlantic coasts, of which the Welsh morfeydd are a part, form a significant proportion of the 5.5 million hectares worldwide. All of them are now threatened by climate change, but the tale of Cwm Ivy is a wonderful note of hope in the light of the inevitability of further sea level rise. The resilience inherent in natural ecosystems, when paired with foresighted land management, can lead to rich outcomes, even if there is pain in the change: will some coastal strips that have never been salt marsh before become new salt marshes in a hundred years, replacing those that are lost?

'The most surprising thing about the marsh,' says Will, 'and what people never believe when I tell them, is that it's not wet! The turf there is much drier than you'd think it would be, because it just naturally drains so quickly.' So when they go down to round the sheep up before the tide comes in, neither they nor the sheep are worried about getting bogged down. But both they and the dogs need to make quick work of it to round all the sheep up before the waters cover the marsh with each tide. It's a case of beeping the horns, running the dogs out and rounding the sheep up. Today they're moved onto an infield on the slope below the castle. A few lambs that have been down on the marsh since April are separated and put up into a field higher up; these ones will be taken to the abattoir to be slaughtered, and their carcasses returned later on to the butchery on the farm.

Will has been up at the farmhouse all morning, serving customers, cutting meat, packing lamb up for delivery. The farm sells meat to passing visitors – many of whom come initially to visit the castle, which although part of the farm, is cared for and marketed as a tourist destination by Cadw, the historic buildings agency of the Welsh government. But they also sell their lamb, along with a neighbouring farm, Bankside, under the brand name 'Gower Salt Marsh Lamb' to local butchers, restaurants and online. With the sheep back up from the marsh and the urgent orders seen to, they all have lunch together in the farmhouse (today's fare was fish and chips). Then there are all the general farm jobs to see to on this farm that comes as close to mixed farming as any – growing crops (fodder beet), hay, ploughing, sowing – depending on the time of year. The farm has 200 acres of dry land, which is more or less organically managed. 'We're not desperate to get certification,' says Will, 'we used to be part of a "pasture-fed" scheme, but it wasn't worth it in the end. It's just some of the silage that isn't organic – but the sheep spend most of the year grazing the marsh anyway, which is as organic as it gets!' Later, there might be a little time left to tackle the list of farm maintenance jobs – fencing, vehicles, machinery. Or to check supplies and make sure the medicines are up to date.

What's their favourite part of farming I ask in the farmhouse kitchen? The reply comes as expected; 'Oh, everything!' Someone else interjects from across the room, 'Rowland's a typical farmer – he wouldn't do anything else!' When pressed, and after a pause to think, the answer takes us back out to the saltmarsh; 'Bringing the sheep off the marsh, you know when you've got them all and the whole flock is running together, and in the right direction – that's special.'

When I taste the lamb itself later on at home, I find that Will is right in how he'd described it. He'd advised me to prepare the chops very simply – just a little salt and pepper, left slightly rare. 'Don't kill it with other flavours.' As he'd said, the meat isn't particularly salty, despite common expectations that it will be because of the salt-marshes and the plants the sheep graze; what really stands out is the distinctly fresh, earthy flavour it has, almost reminiscent of asparagus.

Their meat had in fact recently been tested against lowland Welsh lamb sold in a supermarket at the food technology centre at Cardiff Metropolitan University, and a report then written on it, which Will showed me. Six samples of the salt-marsh lamb from two different cuts were prepared and analysed for appearance, internal characteristics, aroma, odour and texture, both raw and cooked, while the cooked cuts only were also tested for taste. The salt marsh lamb came off very well. The cooked texture in the breakdown is described in the report as being overall 'more succu-lent', with a firmer texture to the meat, which 'maintains integrity during chewing'. The fat had more caramelization compared to the supermarket lamb, and upon eating 'melt[ed] in the mouth'.

The lowland lamb was found to be 'meatier, with an intense lamb aroma', and panellists all picked up on a more metallic aftertaste. The overall conclusions were flattering to the salt-marsh lamb, to say the least: 'The salt marsh lamb was visually more appealing, the texture whilst eating was preferred and the flavour found to be fresher, sweeter, herbier and more rounded.'

It is not surprising then to learn that the internet side of the business has grown enormously over the past few years, and is now by far the biggest single source of income for the farm, and is still growing. The premise is simple: salt-marsh lamb delivered directly through the post to individuals overnight throughout the season, which lasts from the end of June through to Christmas. And they have, over the past few years, started selling mutton again, returning to older patterns of flock management. Unsure whether there would be demand, in 2019 they slaughtered a dozen sheep, advertised Gower mutton and waited to see whether it would sell; it all went. Repeat performances in 2020 and 2021 confirmed that the Welsh taste for mutton hasn't disappeared, and so mutton for this farm, at least, is here to stay.

Perhaps the wiles of fashion which once pushed mutton off our plates can reverse enough to bring it back. My mother made us *cawl cig oen* with saltmarsh lamb once. It was delicious, but you couldn't help feeling that the meat was ultimately too good for cawl. That, however, is very much a matter of opinion. *Cawl cig oen* at its best, made with Welsh lamb or mutton, is a culinary delight, and the continuation of a heritage that marries two of Wales's most deeply rooted and resilient gastronomic traditions; meat broth and rearing sheep. Most Welsh families still have their own cawl recipe, handed down from generation to generation. Cawl is a family tradition and a farmhouse tradition, dependent on the continuation in some form of the long sheep-rearing tradition of this country. That tradition has already changed form numerous times to adapt. Changing demands for wool and changing tastes for lamb have both led to new ways of rearing and eating sheep, and goats have disappeared off Welsh menus entirely. It surely can have a future then, even with demands that sheep numbers be reduced, and for woodland regeneration in the hills. Perhaps that future will require further change – back to mutton and hogget, and even goat. Cawl is simply too good a food and too tasty, and sheep rearing too well-adapted to this land to imagine that Welsh palates and opinion will allow either to disappear.

Yr Halaenwr

Cefais o hoywdrais hydraul
Cofl hallt er mwyn cyfliw haul ...

Dyfod, anrhyfeddod fu.
O dom ardd i dŷ mawrddu;
Sefyll a'r cawell syfudr
Dan fonau 'neufraich, baich budr;
Crio halaen, gaen gwnsallt,
Croyw hoffi cryw heli hallt ...

Deuthum â'r cawell trum cau
Ar fy nghefn, oer fy nghofau,
Hyd i mewn, hoed amynedd,
Hundy gwen, hoendeg o wedd.
Cyfeirio'r ferch ar erchwyn,
Cyfarch gwell i'r ddiell ddyn ...

Hael y cawn gan hoywliw caen
Hwyl, ac nid gwerthu halaen ...

Madog Benfras (fl. 1340)

I bore, costly compulsion
A load of salt for my sun ...

I went, it was a wonder,
From dunghill to great dark house,
Stood with the nasty basket
Under my arms, filthy load,
Shouting 'salt!', shoulders coated
Clear praise of salt-water salt

I entered with the basket
On my back, foolish my thoughts,
Into, passion was patient,
Her bedroom, beautiful girl.
I went to the girl's bedside,
I greeted the sweet one well.
From the fair of skin, kindness
I gave, and not selling of salt …

5

HALEN / SALT

It is autumn 1580. A stiff south-westerly is roaring in off the sea, as it usually does this time of year, reddening cheeks and lacing the air with more than a hint of salt. The men are still at work; two inside the salthouse shovelling coal for the furnace, another hard at work by one of the outside cisterns, trying to re-lime a wall before the winter storms. Smoke wafts out of the panhouse chimneys and is whipped up and away to be mingled with the smoke rising from the cottages in the village behind. The place feels elemental: fire, coal, wind, sea and salt.

This is Port Eynon salthouse, on the south coast of Gower, one of the larger, industrial scale salt production facilities in Wales. It is perfectly situated for its purpose, lying only a few metres above the high-tide line next to a beach now thronged each summer with holi-daymakers. There was another salthouse away at the north-western point of Gower, and several others dotted around the Welsh coast: off the northern shore of Anglesey near Holyhead lies 'Salt island', where sea salt was produced until 1775. On the Menai straits lies the small town of Felinheli – the brine-mill, and a few miles further south lies the town of Pwllheli – the brine pool. It is not surprising that people have produced sea salt along the Welsh coast since time immemorial, given the length of the coastline. But rather than survival or renaissance, the tale of Welsh sea salt production, which might conceivably have led to the sort of long-term success enjoyed by the salterns on the southern coast of Brittany, or even those on the eastern coast of England (exemplified by the well-known Maldon sea salt of Essex) is a story of great potential that, until recently, has never been fully realized.

Salt is the strangest of foodstuffs in a way. Necessary for life, but a modern killer. A harsh, domineering flavour; but, in other contexts, an undetectable flavour enhancer. Extracted from the sea, but also mined from mountains. Used both as a currency and a condiment. Salt has always been valued across the world's civilisations for its ability to preserve foods that would otherwise quickly deteriorate, and now for its ability to bring out the flair in everything from chocolate to chilli.

Salt intake in Wales in the early 21st century is a fair bit higher than public health experts tell us it should be.[1] This is nothing new; from the 20th century's ubiquitous fish and chips to highly salted butter and salted meats and fish, Welsh food has long been known and remarked upon for its saltiness. And the most obvious source for this salt throughout history has been the seas that wash the land of Wales on three sides. Early salterns have been uncovered by archaeological work along part of the British coast, including Iron Age ones with some quite sophisticated ovens built into the ground.[2] This was an obvious way to gain access to this vital condiment and although it is next to impossible to prove that sea salt production occurred in the country in pre-Roman times, by the time of the Roman occupation numerous sites were in operation around the coast of Great Britain.[3]

One interesting early vantage point from which to look at salt and its importance in the story of Welsh food is through the lenses of a poem, 'Yr Halaenwr' (the saltman) written by Madog Benfras from Marchwiail in modern-day Wrexham, who was active c.1340–70.[4] The word *poem* here means something different to what modern readers of English will understand from it. Madog's society was hierarchical and aristocratic; his culture was self-consciously rooted in its own history. He is thus introduced as:

Madog Benfras ap Gruffudd ap Iorwerth, arglwydd Sonlli, ab Einion Goch ab Ieuaf ap Llywarch ap Ieuaf ap Niniaw ap Cynfrig ap Rhiwallawn[5]

– 'Madog Benfras son of Gruffudd son of Iorwerth, Lord of Sonlli, son of Einion the Red, son of Ieuaf son of Llywarch son of Ieuaf son of Niniaw son of Cynfrig son of Rhiwallawn'. In this society, poetry had an important social function, and poets were professionals. It was a high-status activity, codified into strict metres and concerned with singing the praises of noble men, their lavish hospitality and their exploits. It says something then of the grudging respect in which saltmen must have been held in medieval Welsh society – and by extension, of the importance of salt – for this poem to have been written and performed in the first place. Only grudging respect, though, because this was not a high-status occupation in hierarchical medieval societies, with saltmen conspicuously absent from Welsh court rolls, in contrast to the servants responsible for looking after the honey.[6]

'Yr Halaenwr' is in truth a love poem, like most of Madog's poems, with the figure of the saltman being a foil onto which the poet can project his amorous devices. The poem itself is comical, the main idea being that the poet, a member of the upper classes, disguises himself as a saltman (peasant class) in order to win over his unsuspecting lover and gain entry to her bed. But in passing, we learn a lot about saltmen during the poet's era, from their clothing (a leather apron and an old cap) to the saltpans they carried. And despite everything, Madog isn't too mealy-mouthed about the salt-man and his status in society. Yes, his tools are described twice as *budr* – dirty – but he is also quick to praise the figure of the saltman (and yes ... that is in fact himself in this poem): he is 'yr halaenwr hael', the generous saltman. That word – *hael*, generous – was typically reserved only for kings and patrons in this society. Salt seems then a noble enough thing to allow this nobleman-poet both to take on his persona, his attire, and to shower him with praise.

More pertinently, we glean a number of tidbits about the salt-man's trade. Firstly, his salt comes from the *heli hallt* – from the salty brine. This then might be sea salt, harvested by hand perhaps from the wide and shallow Dee estuary near where Madog lived. Or it might be salt from inland brine pits; *heli* is both the word for sea-water and for brine. We know that there were already extensive salt-works in nearby Cheshire and that there were around 100 'wich' or salt-producing houses around the brine pits in Middlewich in the mid-13th century.[7] Madog could in the latter case be basing his poem on travelling saltmen from Cheshire visiting the north of Wales. But this seems far from certain; there were ample supplies of salt found along the country's long, shallow shoreline much nearer Madog's Denbighshire abode than Middlewich, and the well-documented ethnic tensions between the Welsh and the English at the time make it unlikely Madog would talk of the saltman in such positive terms if his poem's imaginary saltman had been an Englishman from Cheshire.

The *halaenwr* also had certain implements he used, all bearing their own names. He thus had a 'cawell syfudr' – dirty salt-basket and a *cryw* or *dellt* – a latticed pan to use with the seawater. These might be different ways of referring to the same instrument; salt baskets of some sort, probably made of wood. We know that medieval salt pans were smaller than those in later periods – some 60cm by 90cm, and 15cm or so deep.[8] These could have been carried around by saltmen, perhaps on their backs as they went around selling salt, as the poem implies.

These saltmen would have been ubiquitous in medieval Wales, with many of them involved both in salt production on a cottage scale and in selling salt at markets and perhaps door to door. The 1722 Llansteffan manuscript – Llansteffan is a town on the south-west coast near Carmarthen – has a dictionary entry for 'halenwr' that confirms this double function, defining the term as 'a salt-boiler or merchant'. In earlier times, the Caernarfon Court Rolls of 1368 mention a 'Goronwy Halaynour' or Goronwy Saltman, who might have worked the shallow waters near coastal Caernarfon. But processes and implements notwithstanding, 'Yr Halaenwr' shows, above all, the role salt played both in the Welsh economy, and in the imagination. Salt – producing it, trading it, using it – was a part of life. Saltmen were a familiar part of society, and perhaps as a result, the saltman disguise in Madog's poem does the trick. The poem ends in an appropriate amorous way, with salt and sex played off each other:

Hael y cawn gan hoywliw caen
Hwyl, ac nid gwerthu halaen

(I generously received from the fair-faced lady
Sex – not selling of salt)

The seeds of the later mixed story of Welsh sea salt are all present in the case of the medieval *halaenwr*. Firstly, the basic importance of ample salt in Welsh food and cooking, meaning that saltmen were common enough to be used as an image in a comic poem. Secondly, the strong hints we get that the term meant both salt-merchant and salt-boiler. Since there are no brine springs within Wales for making rock-salt, salt-boiling must have therefore happened using sea salt. But thirdly, the presence of outside sources of salt that could be imported and sold in Wales, in competition with native sea salt. Most historic salt production around Wales was carried out on a cottage scale rather than as a commercial enterprise. These salt-making ventures have left their mark on the placenames of the country – in both Welsh and English-speaking parts. These occur almost exclusively in areas where natural tidal pools would have occurred. Seawater is not all that saline – 1 litre will only produce 3.5 grams of salt – and so harnessing areas of naturally occurring evaporation was essential to make the venture worthwhile, on whatever scale it was undertaken. On the northern shore of Gower we find 'Salthouse point' near Crofty. Nearby is 'Salthouse pill', a tidal inlet on the Loughor estuary. Near Aberaeron in Ceredigion lies the small cove of 'Gilfach yr Halen' or the 'salt cove', on a hidden stretch of cove a mile or so from the nearest village: perfect for illicit sea salt production to evade the 18th century salt tax. None of this farmhouse-scale salt making was near sufficient to form the basis for an industry. Those exceptions that did arise, like the salthouse at Port Eynon built by the Lucas family, an old Gower family, came about through a combination of coastline with capital and coal.

Although evaporation using open salt pans near the sea is possible in Wales – and the climate during the Roman era and the Middle Ages was 1–2C warmer than it became during the early modern period – it was always marginal. A cold, wet summer could easily mean that salt production dwindled to hardly anything. But where there were suitable coastal sites that were also near coalfields, as at Gower, there was potential for much more dependable production using coal-powered furnaces. Sea water could be transferred the short distance from the beach using simple pumps, stored in reservoir similar in appearance to salt-pans, and then evaporated in metal pans set over flues heated by the coal-fires.[9] The Port Eynon venture was, in fact, one of the earliest to use coal in this way, fully two centuries before this method became widespread.[10]

Other noblemen with access to capital and land saw the opportunities this offered, and turned their hand to similar schemes at other areas around the coast, including near Holyhead and Newport. There was a dramatically ill-fated venture to produce sea salt on a mass scale on the shores of the Dyfi in mid-Wales in the 1560s.[11] Here, fifteen acres of marshland were to be cut up into salt-pans, with a building a hundred and twenty feet long constructed on the edge of the pans to store the salt and for furnaces which were to allow for salt production when the sun wasn't shining. A German, Christopher Schultz, was brought in to oversee the enterprise, and a team of men employed to get it all going. A group of merchants visiting the site in 1569 complained about the poor production practices, with a hundred barrels of salt spoiling that summer due to the practice of measuring the product in an open field. But then the entire enterprise disappears from the record, perhaps partly as a result of geopolitical changes in the relationship between England and France, meaning that French salt could again be sold at profit in Britain. The floodgates were opened, and developing a new salt-works on the west coast of Wales became unprofitable. No matter, in one sense; the Welsh had their salt.

Salted

Even if salt making was progressing only in fits and starts, salt was essential and widely used. It was used, as elsewhere in Europe, to preserve foods of all sorts for the winter. Herring was salted in large quantities around the coast, and throughout the country every household would spend time in autumn salting ham, mutton, beef and occasionally other foods. The knowledge of how to use salt for preservation was taken for granted, and no household would have survived for long without it. The wars of conquest that ravaged medieval Wales throw this into sharp relief, as soldiers and others were sometimes subjected to long sieges in the castles built in almost every corner of the country. In Neath in 1316, the garrison was besieged for 58 days; in their storerooms, alongside 120 bushels of wheat, 32 of oats, 12 sides of pig and 1,000 gallons of beer, they were amply supplied with 104 bushels of salt.[12]

The story of *cig moch* – the Welsh term that encompasses both ham and bacon – goes a long way to exemplifying the importance of salt. If beef brought wealth, and sheep dominated the hills, then pigs were the household companion throughout Wales well into the twentieth century. The Welsh love of pigs was legendary, as numerous travellers from over Offa's Dyke couldn't help remarking: 'we could not avoid observing the number of pigs, which are esteemed in this country far superior to any in England'.[13] Pigs, known for their intelligence, and valued for their meat, were treated royally as a result: 'these are noble animals in Wales, of a large, majestic breed. The hog in highland regions is generally considered one of the family, and is very commonly seen reposing comfortably before the cottage fire with the children sporting about him.'[14] This native Welsh breed of pig – compact, pink-skinned and of a famously friendly disposition – is memorably described by Dorothy Hartley:

Llani Wild loaf made with Felin Ganol wholemeal flour.
© Carwyn Graves

Felin Ganol with its waterwheel on the Afon Wyre.
© Carwyn Graves

Cheesemaking equipment handed down from the late
19th century at Glyneithinog farm (Caws Cenarth).

© Carwyn Graves

Rounds of Caerffili cheese ripening in the 'cave' at Glyneithinog.

© *Carwyn Graves*

'Caws bobi' (Welsh rarebit), as served in restaurants today.

Seaweed (laver) drying huts at Freshwater West beach (Pembs) in the 1930s.
These were built by local women from driftwood and marram grass thatch.
Unknown photographer

Gathering cockles in Penclawdd, Glamorgan,
for sale in the town markets of south Wales, 1951.

Cattle Llannerch-y-medd fair in the 1880s, which
attracted drovers from far and wide.

© National Library of Wales

Sheep on an infield at Weobley Castle farm, with the saltmarshes behind.

© Carwyn Graves

David Lee-Wilson, co-founder of Halen Môn, using his refractometer to inspect the saltiness of the waters in the Menai Strait, Anglesey.
© *Maria Bell Photography*

Sea salt crystals being processed at Halen Môn's site on the Anglesey shoreline.
© *Maria Bell Photography*

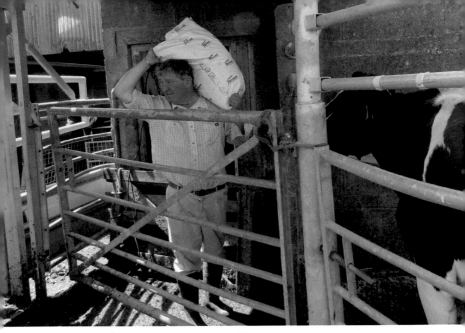

John Lougher on his way to attend to one of the cows at Tŷ Tanglwyst farm.

© *Carwyn Graves*

Maggie Edwards, Llanfechell c. 1880, posing for tea (one of many food innovations in Wales) in Welsh traditional dress.

© *National Library of Wales*

Alex Simmens in his orchard at Llanblethian
with trugs of harvested perry pears.

© *Carwyn Graves*

The wildlife-friendly orchard aglow in the September sun.

© *Carwyn Graves*

A traditional stone cider mill. There were at least 150 of these
in south-eastern Wales in the early 20th century. This one is
at St Fagans National Museum of History, Cardiff.

© Richard Downs / Alamy Stock Photo

Cardiff's Caroline Street – known as 'Chippy Lane' or 'Chip Alley' – serving the
good folk of the city with golden fried potatoes as it has done for over 140 years.

© Steve Morgan at Juno's View blog

Paul Griffiths with a witty word and homecooked food on a busy
Saturday at the Cabin in Ferryside, Carmarthenshire.

A potato patch near a housing estate in north-east Wales,
at a time when significantly more food was locally produced.

© *National Library of Wales*

A bowl of my Mam's homemade mutton cawl, with
plenty of 'stars on its face', as it should have.

© Carwyn Graves

Sioni Winwns in their lodgings and onion storehouse
in Porthmadog in the 1950s.

© *National Library of Wales*

'As all animals in the principality, he is comparatively small. Little but good. He has been kept by every Welsh miner, quarryman and farmer, for centuries. Foraging free round the hillside in youth, he develops activity and sagacity. He is a "good doer" for his small self, and later, in the small stone sties, he fattens quickly on household waste, in nice time for the Christmas pork and winter bacon ... Note the mild Welsh leek and wild sage of his mountain environment are his natural accompaniments.'[15] This valuable and docile native breed of pig is now classified as being 'at risk' by the Rare Breeds Survival Trust.

That range of foods – both household waste and what could be had scrounging on the hillsides – undoubtedly contributed to the succulence of the pork. Pigs roamed free in deer parks across medieval Wales, fattening themselves up in the oak woods ahead of being slaughtered to keep households in meat for the winter. This custom, called pannage in English and *mesobr* in Welsh, was widely known across northern Europe, and was an important means for local populations to skim the resources produced by woodlands and uncultivated hillsides, and convert that bounty into useable food. The Welsh season for *mesobr* as recorded in 1722 lasted from 25 September until 1 November – slightly later than in adjacent parts of southern England. This method of raising pigs produces meat that is much deeper and richer in both colour and flavour than modern supermarket pork, which is pale and insipid in comparison.

When pig slaughtering day came in late autumn, it was time to call in the neighbours for help. No part of the animal could be wasted, and even the flowing blood would be caught in a bowl for use in cooking later that day. Some would be given to the neighbours, and these gifts in kind would be reciprocated when their pig-killing day came around a week or two later.[16] My grandfather recalled, with a laugh, that, in his day the pig would be slaughtered in the same bath-tub generally used for washing the children. In my grandfather's family, poor cottagers in the Preseli hills in the depression of the 1930s, things had to be put to multiple uses.

'Everybody had to have a pig. In many a village there was more discussion about pigs after chapel on a Sunday morning than there was about the sermon!' In a piece of oral history captured in the 1970s, George Tucker, a Gower builder, shared similar recollections of childhood ways in his village in the 1890s. 'Reports, comparisons, my grandfather used to tell me: "if anybody asks you to guess the weight of his pig, always judge 'em high, you'll be their friend for life". Some butchers used to kill 'em standing up, but with a big pig that was a nasty job. You've got your pig now on his side, with three or four fellows now lying on him, and the butcher would stick him, under the throat … The next thing was scraping the pig, then you'd hang him up.' Different parts of the pig were then put apart for various uses: the innards, the gut, the ears, trotters and tail. But then came the salting to make the ham: 'You'd put the bacon down, the hams on top of the bacon, with salt and a bit of salt-petre around the knuckle, that's where it would go first. Then after three weeks, you'd wash it off and hang it up in the charnel to dry, one ham each side of the fire and the flitches up in the charnel. And that would last a small cottager twenty score [i.e. forever and a day], you see … well, till a pig come again.'

This tradition of making hams, common to all the British Isles in some form, continued to be more widespread in Wales than England, where the fashion was shifting to pickling meats from the 18th century.[17] Only the York ham was still cured in the older way by salting and hanging, and it retained a reputation among the

London classes because of it. The Welsh ham tradition is therefore noteworthy for its different development path to the majority of English hams, which are often cured in brine, treacle or honey. It is in fact much more similar to the much better known classic air-dried hams of the continent, such as the celebrated Italian *prosciutto di Parma* or the Spanish *jamon serrano*.

Serrano hams are hung for 18 months in the dry, mountainous Extremadura mountains. The Welsh Carmarthen ham – produced to this day and available at the town's covered market – hangs for a shorter period of 6–9 months, and in the moister conditions of western Wales, with its year-round Atlantic breezes. Carmarthen ham has been awarded PGI status as the last regional survival from a formerly widespread tradition of air-dried salt-cured hams. Traditionally, the hams would hang for as long as necessary until they were needed; some would be eaten as soon as three to four weeks after salting, and others would be left until the following spring. One local recalls that his mother claimed she could forecast the weather by examining the salt moisture on the sides of bacon.

Salt was thus the essential, key ingredient that allowed these traditions to develop. The mouth-feel of a Carmarthen ham today is memorable, with an initially smooth, slightly sweet tang followed by a sublime moment as the salt bites the palate, cutting through the other sensations. The initial delicate, flaky texture gives way perceptibly to softer, slightly fruity pork notes. Eaten on a slice of malty bread, this is a small taste of heaven.

But there is little to suggest that these hams and bacons were mostly eaten cold; rather, they were one of the workhorses of Welsh cooking, combined with eggs, cockles, potatoes and various vegetables in numerous ways and always bringing with them a burst of fatty, salty flavour. Bacon and cabbage was a common dish in many parts, as was the delectable *cig moch, caws a winwns* – bacon, cheese and onions: bacon rashers covered with thick slices of cheese on top of a thick layer of chopped onion, covered and baked in a slow oven. Variants of this existed with liver instead of cheese, common in north-west Wales, or as *Tatws Pum Munud* (five minute potatoes), where bacon, potato and onion are seasoned, covered with a small amount of boiling water and cooked until the water is absorbed and the potatoes turn golden brown.[18]

Despite its ubiquity, the salt used for these hams across Wales was often of French provenance. It was French production, even more so than Cheshire rock salt, that seems to have been responsible for the fact that, despite promising starts to Welsh efforts to produce sea salt at scale for the market, nothing much came of the various ventures. Indeed, despite the multiple advantages of clean seas, a long coastline, ample fuel and native know-how, Wales remained a net importer of salt down the centuries – with the exception of small-scale, illicit cottage production. Precisely because of salt's importance as a foodstuff and preserver, it has long been highly regulated and seen as an important source of tax revenue for governments. The English Domesday Book records in minute detail all the salt-production sites around the coast of early Norman England, and, for similar reasons, the salthouses at Port Eynon and at Holyhead were fortified.[19] As a result, salt production and import were both highly regulated, with salt excise officers employed at ports all around Wales.

French coastal salt production sites had been running without interruption and at some scale since the Roman era, and were able to produce enough to export to those parts of northern Europe – including Wales – where solar evaporation was more marginal. There are thus ample records of salt imports into Welsh ports throughout the Middle Ages, presumably supplementing what was produced locally.[20] Given that many upper-class businessmen at various times had commercial interests in this import trade, and that government had a strong interest in regulating the trade at all times, there was little incentive or freedom generally for Welsh coastal dwellers to develop sea salt production. The exceptions to this, such as the late 16th century, when both Port Eynon and the Dyfi site were developed, came about because of interruptions to the supply from France because of war or other geopolitical difficulties – and so led to government encouragement of new salt works. As is widely recognized, government policy, and the economic possibilities which this enables or thwarts, can lead to entire industries either flourishing or floundering, and the Welsh sea salt industry (or lack of it) seems to be a clear test case for this. Sea salt production is thus perhaps the most frustrating tale of undeveloped potential both in this book and in the long story of Welsh food.

Halen Môn

But sometimes, a spluttering start is an unfair harbinger for what is to come. Just over the Menai straits from the mountains of Snowdonia is Wales's largest modern-day sea salt producer, Halen Môn (Anglesey salt). The brainchild of a couple who had come to Wales to study at nearby Bangor University, Halen Môn has become one of the most widely recognised Welsh food products, is now used as an ingredient in luxury foods ranging from cheese to caramel and has inspired numerous other small-scale sea salt producers around Wales.

Alison and David Lea-Wilson had started out in business selling oysters. Their fishmonger's business gradually became a fish exhibitor's business (Anglesey Sea Zoo, which is still next door to

Halen Môn's saltcote), which gave them their first real encounter with sea salt from the Menai straits, a stone's throw from their site. This came about, as they will readily tell you, through sea horses. Sea horses only thrive in extremely pure, unpolluted sea water, and the fact that the seahorses at their sea zoo were thriving suggested to them that the briny waters of the Menai might well produce a high-quality sea salt. Their first experiments in making sea salt to sell came about primarily because of the seasonality of the sea zoo enterprise. Wanting to be able to run a profitable business year-round, they quickly fell upon the idea of making sea salt. At the time, no new sea salt company had been founded anywhere in the British Isles for 125 years, so they started on a small scale. Their first customer was the local butcher, Swain's of Menai Bridge (which still sells the salt today). They gradually earnt themselves a reputation, and the business grew quickly. Halen Môn's success has blazed a trail that numerous others have since followed across the British Isles.

Being perfectionists, they decided from the outset to try and produce the highest quality salt they could manage. David spent a couple of years going round the world to find ways to improve the salt. When a pan of seawater is boiled, the product left over once the water has evaporated is salt. But this salt is typically not only composed of sodium chloride, a highly stable compound, but also calcium carbonate – chalk – which has a bitter aftertaste. Alison and David were keen to find a way of producing salt economically without calcium carbonate.

They eventually fell upon a process that worked to their satisfaction. The seawater is extracted from the Menai straits through pipes (and since these pipes cross the foreshore, a fee must be paid to the Crown Estate for the privilege) and pumped at high tide into tanks. This water is then filtered using charcoal and sand. After this, the pure seawater is boiled in flasks – so that the process is more energy-efficient – at a boiling point of around 80C. The distilled water – i.e. the steam – is then captured, bottled and sold as such. The remaining salt is shovelled into trays with warm water, where it is allowed to crystallize. It's at this point that the salt is rinsed in a brine concentration so that the calcium carbonate goes back into the water, leaving pure sodium chloride. What the salt loses in volume it gains in quality and flavour. This pure sea salt then spends 24–26 hours in an oven at low temperatures to dry out completely, before being packed by hand.

It isn't just snobbery to prefer sea salt to rock salt produced from inland brine springs: the two types of salt are chemically different. Although at base composed of sodium chloride, numerous other trace elements are present in naturally produced salt. In the case of sea salt made from the waters of the North Atlantic, as here, there can be up to 80 of these different elements present, including magnesium, calcium, potassium, iron, zinc and iodine. Each of these plays an essential role in human health, for example, magnesium in cell and brain function, calcium in bone formation and iodine in cell metabolism. The presence of these elements gives the salt a stronger but also less harsh flavour, meaning a smaller amount goes further on food.

Halen Môn has successfully emphasised this fact in two decades of marketing. By 2019, half a million packets of this salt were packed annually by the company, with 38% of these going to other EU countries, primarily Spain, Italy and Sweden. The rest is sold either to individuals through their website and other stockists, or wholesale to other companies in north Wales and beyond; companies such as Jones Crisps, South Caernarfon Creameries – who make cheddar – and Green & Black's chocolate. They have also been ever-ready to try out new ways of selling salt – for instance, Halen Môn was the first company to start selling smoked salt in the UK. They installed a smokery on site, which burns oak, hickory, apple-wood or others at customer request. Despite its slightly gimmicky feel, the salt tastes good, and it's not hard to imagine how it could benefit a wet summer barbecue that had to be finished off in the oven … or just plump, ripe tomatoes, perhaps.

But despite their success in finding all sorts of buyers for their salt and in creating spin-off products like the smoked salt or fla-voured salt, it's the pure, crisp, startling-white sea salt itself that interests me. Happily, the company wears its confidence in its salt on its sleeve. When I visit, they bring out a number of different salts for me to compare in a taste test: 'table salt' (which is a rock salt with 5% anti-caking agent); pure rock salt; a grey sea salt from France; pure Halen Môn, and then their more recent innovation, oak-smoked salt. The table salt tastes harsh and vaguely unpleasant; it feels like it would only suit cheap oven chips or salt and shake crisps. The rock salt is slightly better, but definitely gritty. The grey salt is a definite step up, and not bad at all; but the Halen Môn is markedly more pleasant in flavour, with a roundedness and a deli-cate crispiness the others just don't have.

This is perhaps fitting, given their home on Wales's largest island, surrounded by the clean Irish Sea on three sides, and the Menai straits on the other. The windswept isle of Anglesey, whose low-lying, rocky, sandy coastline is more reminiscent of Brittany than mainland Wales, has long been home to notable fishing and seafaring traditions. The ports of Holyhead and Amlwch together land an annual catch worth over £4 million, making them easily the largest ports in northern Wales. The Menai straits, the swift-flowing tidal 'river' that divides the island from the mainland – and was first crossed by bridge in 1826 – is also home to one of the largest mussel farms in the UK today. Halen Môn sits a hundred yards back from the foreshore of the straits, near the point where it opens out into Caernarfon Bay, with views across to mighty Caernarfon castle and the mountains of Snowdonia beyond. To the south, the sweep of Caernarfon Bay rises up to the three peaks of the Eifl hills on the northern end of the Llŷn peninsula. Unlike many parts of southern Wales, or the coastlands of the Dee estuary towards the English border, there is no industry on these shores, nor the scars of any past industry larger in scale than fishing or limework.

But an unspoilt landscape is only half the story. This was formerly a rich island, targeted by the Roman legions of 2,000 years ago because of its importance as the headquarters of Druidic religion. Later, the island's sunny, drier climate and erstwhile fertile soils made it the breadbasket of the medieval kingdom of Gwynedd and earnt it the epithet of 'Môn Mam Cymru' – Anglesey, mother of Wales. But today the island as a whole counts by most measures as one of the most economically deprived parts of rural Wales, and amongst the poorest parts of the entire UK. It has an economy based almost exclusively on tourism and livestock farming and the public sector has steadily dwindled and found itself in a vicious cycle, as young people move away, and are replaced by pensioners from off the island.

With this in mind, I ask one of Halen Môn's 23 employees how they would describe the company. The reply comes without hesitation: 'ethical'. 'Just ethical across the board. They [Alison and David] really care about us. There are things they could do mechanically, and save money by doing so, but they don't in order to give more of us work. They've just opened a café here, and employed a young chef just starting out in the trade. And though they don't speak it fluently, they are so supportive of the language, they make it really prominent on our branding – and really do more to support the language and culture here than many native speakers do.'

It strikes me as I leave the island that the story of Welsh sea salt production is a curious one. With over one and a half thousand miles of coastline (compared to only 160 miles of land border with England) of every shape and description, clean seas and a strong taste for salty food, and a ready supply of fuel for those occasional cloudy days, the conditions were present for an early and success-ful Welsh sea salt industry. That this didn't really happen until the 20th century says much about how government policy – as well as wider economic conditions – can do much to hamper sens-ible development. There is here a valuable lesson in assessing the past: sometimes the near misses are as instructive as the runaway successes.

Ffoles Llantrisant

Mae gen i stwc, mae gen i hilydd
Mae gen i fuddai fechan newydd

Cytgan:
Mae gen i ffansi fawr iawn i dy garu,
Pe cawn i lonydd gan y diogi.

Mae gen i iâr, mae gen i geiliog,
Mae gen i gywan felan focho

(Cytgan)

Oer yw'r rhew ac oer yw'r eira,
Oer yw'r ty heb dau yn y Gaeaf

(Cytgan)

Du yw y nos, du yw y Gaeaf,
Duach na du yw 'nghalon inne

(Cytgan)

Hyfryd yw gweld yr haul yn y bore
Pan fydd y byd i gyd ar ei ore

(Cytgan)

Llantrisant Fancies

I have a cask, I have a strainer
and my churn lying a-ready

Chorus:
I've a great fancy to love you
If only I could stop idling about

I have a hen, I have a cockerel
and my chubby, yellow chicklet

(Chorus)

Cold the frost, cold the snow
Cold the house for one in winter

(Chorus)

Black the night, black the winter
Blacker still my heart

(Chorus)

The morning sun's a joy to see
And all the world at its best

(Chorus)

Folk Song from Glamorgan collected in 1844.

6

MENYN / BUTTER

I am walking up a trackway under the noonday sun, thick hedge-rows on either side. Over the hedge to my left are a couple of deep green fields, bordered by a bright oakwood. I can hear the cows, sheltering under some mature ash trees slightly behind me, their wet breathing echoing against the sound of my boots on the dust as I trudge uphill. As I walk, I reflect on the fact that this land has worn so much of the form it now wears for centuries, and in part millennia. This takes my breath away slightly: cows have been grazing and sitting in the shade under ash trees in hedge-lined fields in this part of the world for as far back as records go, and beyond.

I am on the land of Tŷ Tanglwyst farm, some two miles inland from the Glamorgan coast, and am on my way up to see the Iron Age hill fort in Tŷ Tanglwyst woods. The woman's name Tanglwyst is rarely heard in Wales today, so the very name of the place – Tanglwyst's house – evokes antiquity and societies that are no more. But at the same time, for the people who live around here the antiquity in this landscape that I am reflecting on is so easy to take for granted, to dismiss as a triviality, even though it is in many ways just as remarkable as the celebrated ancient olive groves of Greece or Israel. Two thousand years ago, much of modern Germany was untouched forest. A thousand years ago, the now hedge-lined English Midlands were open countryside, more similar in feel to parts of the American Midwest in their openness than to their current form. Five hundred years ago, the now empty Scottish glens were full of homesteads and scattered villages, emptied and transformed to make way for sheep. But in this and many other parts of the Welsh countryside, some of the current fields, tracks and settlements were already recognizable in the Iron Age, and the oldest field systems are believed to date back to the Bronze Age. This, and the fact that many of these fields were set out expressly for cattle, not unrelated to the ones I see here today, seems to me quite remarkable.

Those cattle would also have been grazing meadows made up of an abundance of grassland species. On a lazy July day like this one, when the air is heavy with the humming of insects and laced with the lightest of breezes, you can in these parts of the world sometimes taste the herbs on the wind. A field of grass is much more than it seems, and the same buttercups that children hold up to chins, the daisies that form chains and crowns and the orchids that now draw protection at sites of special scientific interest: all form part of an ecosystem long primed for making butter. Butter, that golden delight, depends on rich creamy milk. And milk of that sort needs good grazing country, which is precisely what this is. Thanks to the abundant rainfall and a mild climate all year round away from the mountainous interior, a good proportion of Wales is excellent butter country and has long been recognized as such.

John Evans, a travel writer visiting the country in 1804, wrote that 'the excellency of Glamorgan butter is too well known to need any eulogy … Great quantities are annually salted and exported to Bristol and other places. This article of luxury seems to have been invented by the natives.' This Glamorgan butter was, of course, salted. Salt belongs in dairy – or such, at least, has always been the case in Wales. And salty butter, in particular, spread generously on a chunk of fresh, crusty bread, is one of the inimitable tastes of home for a native of Wales (as it is, I'm told on good authority, for a Breton or a native of Ireland). Salt was added to butter as a preservative from prehistoric times. The salt content in butter varied traditionally across Europe; in Normandy, the local Isigny butter traditionally has a salt content of 2%, whilst in most parts of Germany most butter has been unsalted since the Middle Ages, as a result of salt taxes. In Wales, surrounded by a ready source of illicit salt in the sea on three sides, people were able to keep their predilection for salty butter; a common benchmark today is 3.5%.

Butter is the product of churning cream, and was traditionally made on the majority of farms or smallholdings throughout the country. A product valued wherever it was made for its flavour, keeping properties and high fat content, butter seems to have been held in particularly high regard in the Celtic countries. In Ireland, it was used as a form of currency, and for many poorer people would have been one of the main sources of income and dietary fat. William Camden's description of Britain, *Britannia*, published in 1586, makes a point of describing the diet of the population of mountainous north-west Wales, so different in language and culture to his native London; 'the inhabitants for most part wholy betake themselves to breeding and seeding of cattail, and live upon white meates, as butter, cheese &c'. This upland, pastoral economy, far from meaning that the population lived in poverty, formed the basis for not insubstantial wealth. The basis of this was cattle, with, as we've seen, the beef export market being the main source of income. One of the greatest concentrations of well-built medieval and sub-medieval farmhouses in Wales lies in Snowdonia, with houses like Gwastadannas, Nantgwynant or Egryn, Llanaber visible manifestations of prosperity.[1] But while the cattle were exported, their produce – what was known at the time as 'white meats', and particularly the cheese and butter – were of vital importance in people's diets.

Early visitors to Wales remarked on the plentiful butter they found there. A visitor to Carmarthen in 1652 described it as 'one of the plentifullest townes that I ever set my foot in, for very fair egs are cheaper than small pears'. He goes on to list the prices he found for various foodstuffs at the town market, including, 'butter as good as the world affords, two pence halfepenney, for three pence the pound'. Similarly, a contemporary observer says of the food of Flintshire in the north-east in 1695, 'fruits are not very common; but of milk, butter, cheese and honey there is plenty'. Along with other dairy products, butter seems to have been ubiquitous in historic Welsh diets.

A farmhouse culture grew up around butter, and alongside the distinguishing mark of high salt content, a notable feature of Wales's butter making culture is the now mostly forgotten tradition of butter presses, or moulds. Each farm or dairy had its own wooden press, used to stamp the name or mark of the farm onto a slab of butter – effectively fulfilling the same function as a label or logo today. These presses are objects of beauty, often inscribed with the pattern of a thistle, a leaf, or other natural objects. Hundreds remain on farmhouse mantelpieces and in museums the length and breadth of the country. They testify to a culture in which people cared about the quality of the butter they bought, and where butter makers took pride in marketing their produce as their own.

But with the industrialization of food production in the 19th century, more and more farmhouse production moved to the large local dairies. Then, through the course of the twentieth century, the logic of centralization went further still and there was a marked decline in the number of local dairies in Wales. Refrigeration combined with low transportation costs gave companies that could operate at economies of scale a significant advantage. As was widely the case across northern Europe, milk rounds went from being the customary way of buying fresh milk, to being one option among many, to being a comparative rarity.

Tŷ Tanglwyst

One of the few family farms in Wales that still makes its own butter in its own dairy today is Tŷ Tanglwyst, near Porthcawl on the Glamorgan coast. As Rhys Lougher, the youngest in his family's long line of Glamorgan farmers, explains, 'when we were starting out, there were many more farm dairies like this all over Wales. Many of those have closed in the last ten years or so. What's against us is the economics.'

Four generations of Loughers live on the farm, with its sprawling sub-medieval farmhouse crouching at the centre. Standing in the old orchard behind the house, Rhys's father John points out his grandfather's original dairy at its western end. 'They made butter for themselves, of course – like they had the apples and the pears and the raspberries and all too – but like eight or nine other farms round here, they were getting their money from supplying the town of Porthcawl with its milk. There were no fridges, see, so twice a day they'd go in with milk, morning and evening.' He stops and reflects a moment, as we stand there in the warm mid-summer sun, before going on. 'He had a herd of shorthorns, my grandad did – just twelve cows. Nobody would make a living with twelve cows today.'

John's grandad's grandfather probably also had a similar size herd, as would countless generations of Loughers in this part of the world before him. The farm's 120 acres – which make it a medium-size family farm in today's Wales – lie on good limestone soils, and before the early 20th century would have been regarded as particularly large. Here too though, the Welsh microcosm is in evidence. From the path up to Tŷ Tanglwyst woods you can see north towards the normally cloud-topped *blaenau*, the coal-country of the Glamorgan uplands. There, only a few miles away, annual rainfall totals can be almost twice what they are here, and the cold, thin soils can't support nearly as many livestock. But the coal under the ground paved the way for a boom in population, leading to tightly-packed terraces of miners and factory workers who needed feeding. As your gaze sweeps to the west, you pass Margam Abbey, whose monks owned Tŷ Tanglwyst in the Middle Ages and who left their mark not least in the vaulted chamber underneath the original farmhouse. Due north there is a clear view of the now-threatened towers of Port Talbot steelworks, which more or less created and still sustain that coastal town. That town, in turn and along with others, spawned the neighbouring seaside town of Porthcawl as an August resort for the miners and factory workers. And then immediately west lies the sea, stretching westwards past the cliffs of the Gower coast until at a certain point it becomes the Atlantic.

This view would have been one of the reasons the Iron Age inhabitants of Wales chose to build a small fort on top of this knoll now covered in ancient oaks, ash and hazel. They farmed cattle on this land too of course, with the stealing of cattle one of the primary forms of self-aggrandizement in Celtic society. The Romans left their remains here too, in the form of half a quern, a hand-mill for grain. Of course, the Celts and Romans in question would often have been the same people, even the same individuals. This is a kaleidoscope of continuity and change, and one of the remarkable elements of continuity has been the choice to graze this land with cattle, and to make butter from their rich milk.

But the change comes in the form of economic pressures. Over the course of the twentieth century, like most farms in Wales, the herd size here increased from John's grandad's twelve cows and the economic climate pushed the farm to further specialize in dairy. By the 1990s, the herd was 60 cows strong and supplying the independent creamery in Bridgend with milk. But then Dairy Farmers of Britain, which had ended up running the dairy, went bust. John recalls, 'fifteen milkmen came knocking on our doors the very next morning, more or less! Well, we couldn't take them all on, far from it – but that was the start of it.'

Even before then, economic pressures had pushed them to look into other sources of income. Some of the old, stone farm buildings had been turned into holiday lets. They put some fields down to pick-your-own strawberries: 'that worked and we had lovely strawberries. But then over eight years we saw fewer and fewer customers – it was just when the supermarkets started stocking them all year round and it became unviable.' They looked into cheese too, visited established cheese producers in West Wales and even started tests for producing soft cheese on site – but the storage, the equipment, and the challenge of creating a market were significant obstacles. Creating a market for your product is long, slow work.

Then, when the Bridgend creamery closed, there was suddenly a market for their milk – but it needed to be pasteurized and bottled first. 'Yes, we were catapulted into it a little,' says Rhys with a chuckle, 'and we applied for a grant, and when we got it we thought it was an enormous sum! But it all went just for the capital investment – all the new equipment and facilities we would need if this was going to happen. I mean, you think it's just going one step up the supply chain, it's not going to be so different to what you already know, but in fact it's an entirely different world.'

Rhys and John are likeable, affable men, who are obviously very happy to welcome visitors onto their farm – and it's obvious they are also sharp operators who keep their noses to the ground. The business grew, to the point where they now employ 25 people, making them the largest employer in their village: 'We've now got delivery milkmen, farm hands, production staff who do the pasteurising, three people on the butter. We deliver our milk, cream and butter to shops, cafés, restaurants, patisseries, ice-cream parlours almost all within a 25-mile radius, and most are a lot more local than that. And our milk is also going into all the schools here. That's probably what I am most proud of, because we pushed and pushed for that local procurement from the council. And now, we've got those relationships and the kids come up on class visits, to meet the actual cows that produce their milk.'

They have developed a good brand and they have a good story to tell – one they are proud of. But even so, 'the economics are against us. People want cheap food – cheap milk particularly. My ten-year-old son is into skateboarding in a big way, and he was telling me recently, "Dad, when I take over the farm, I'm going to turn it into a skateboard park." And I can't argue against it – he'll have a better business plan than dairy farming!' I'm struck again by the ludicrousness of this situation that has become normalized: food being so cheap, particularly when produced in cheap ways to be sold at rock-bottom, loss-leader prices, that those whom society depends on to ensure its future can hardly afford to keep their businesses going.

Rhys obviously cares deeply about food and farming, and wants to play his part in educating people about what good farming looks like – like the kids he mentions who come on school visits and don't have a clue that milk comes from cows. And it isn't just the kids whose food education is lacking. He bursts into laughter as he remembers some of the teachers, 'I have had more than one teacher ask me with an entirely straight face "Do you get more milk from the cows or the bulls?" You've got to laugh or you'd cry.'

The cows currently grazing this land are Holsteins, from a long-established herd stewarded and developed for decades by the family. They are a closed herd (bulls are not brought in from outside for breeding), and have won many prizes over the years. And when I ask Rhys about them, he has no hesitation in answering. 'I love working with the cows. Seeing them happy, healthy, carrying the tradition on with the herd. I am genuinely proud of what we do here – I think we have the balance right.'

The cows graze outdoors all the way from early April to early November ('though who knows these days, with the weather changing so much'), but as Rhys emphasizes, it's cow-led and if they want to stay inside because it's hot or wet, they can do that. When I visit on a warm day in high summer, the cows are lazing about in the shade of a tall ash tree. Milk is a complex liquid, comprised of a variety of minerals, proteins, sugars and fats. But it is universally recognized these days that the highest quality milk comes from animals fed their natural diet – fresh green grass, clover, foliage and herbs. Milk from pasture-fed animals is higher in vitamin E, omega 3 fats and conjugated linoleic acids than milk from animals fed other diets.[2] And for a much longer part of the year than would be possible in most parts of northern Europe, these cattle graze the pastures – and even in the winter, eat much of the fossilized goodness of the summer pastures in the form of hay.

The farm system, Rhys tells me, is cyclical, and they are working on it making it more so with each passing year. 'We use the cattle manure itself as fertilizer, and we're growing more clover. And although I'm not an ecologist, it does feel to me like we have a healthy ecosystem here. The insects love the dung pats, we've got owls and sparrowhawks. We have wildflower meadows – like right now, there's one meadow where we have had orchids flowering, so we've not mown it yet. We'll wait till they've set seed before we do that. And we're now making hay again – things have come full circle in a way, back to the way they were in the past.'

He's excited this year because they've grown peas to mix with barley as an arable silage for the cows for the first time. With a smile he tells me about his grandmother, who was out yesterday evening picking them as fast as she could, and his grandfather relegated to shelling duty, preparing the peas for the family's supper, for a good hour. All of that is reducing the farm's dependence on bought-in cereals for feed, which is also helping to cut carbon emissions. Given all this, I ask Rhys whether the farm has considered becoming organic. He responds with another wry smile. 'It annoys me that a lot of people go organic just to charge the premium. We adopt a lot of the organic principles in what we do anyway – but we couldn't go organic as things are, because there is such a lack of organic grain grown in Wales, and we couldn't sustain the cows through the winter.' The work of the Welsh Grain Forum and their desire to recreate a viable local grain economy in Wales comes to mind. It sounds like the demand could be there, even in the form of animal feed, were the infrastructure built to produce and process grains at scale and at an affordable price.

'But am I for cutting emissions, keeping things local, protecting the wildlife? Just look at my farm! We've also been restoring some more hedges recently as well, to create more wildlife corridors; one of the reasons we can't expand is because the M4 cuts through the country right there', he indicates – two fields down from the farmhouse.

The butter is churned on the farm, twice a week. 'Tuesday and Thursday are our butter days,' Rhys explains, 'and yes, the salt content is 3.5%, as it should be for a Welsh butter. It's been popular ever since we started making it a decade ago. We get shops ringing us up asking to stock it, and we say that they can only stock it if they'll take our milk too' (which is equally good, but bulkier and more perishable). 'We won the Golden Fork for it at the Great Taste awards a couple of years ago – which made us one of the 18 winners out of 10,000 products entered.'

It is perhaps a cliché in a book on food to say that you can taste the quality of the farming, or the artisanship, in the food itself. But the almost-white butter which the Loughers give me to take home, when I taste it, really does have the texture of cream and in its flavour almost a bouquet of vanilla. Although made from pasteurized milk and made in the sweet-cream tradition of the British Isles, rather than the arguably richer continental lactic tradition, this is a butter that you could eat with a (tea)spoon.

Buttery treats

Tŷ Tanglwyst's butter is used by a number of bakeries; unsurprisingly, given how many baked goods depend on a rich butter flavour for their mojo. In fact, the central place of butter in Welsh food culture, stemming from the primarily pastoral farming that has always dominated the country, led to the development of a wide range of offshoots – drinks, alcoholic beverages and almost all of the traditional cakes and treats that crown festivities in Wales. Two of these are 'bara brith' and 'Welsh cakes', the two Welsh 'sweets' par excellence, which depend on good, rich, salty butter for their mouth-filling moreishness.

Bara brith, literally 'speckled bread', is a dark, yeasted fruit loaf, made with currants steeped overnight in black tea, and is most commonly associated with northern Wales. But Welsh cakes – *pice ar y maen* or *pice lap*, or *teisen gri*, depending on which part of the country you come from – are Wales's most iconic teatime treat. A good Welsh cake is lightly browned on top, with an ever so slightly crusty outer layer encompassing the rich, buttery inside. Its texture is hard to describe to those familiar with the dichotomous division of baked goods into cakes and biscuits; it lies somewhere in the middle, with some of the softness of cake, but some of the dense firmness of a biscuit. You hold the end of a Welsh cake between two fingers, and the rest of it won't crumble and fall away like a moist piece of cake would. Although eggs were used in many traditional recipes, it's the richness of good butter that really makes a Welsh cake. In fact, this is true twice over as older recipes contained buttermilk as well, giving a lightly sour undertone to the dough.

Buttermilk itself – *llaeth enwyn* – was ubiquitous in Wales, and as a testament again to the presence of butter in all households and through a good portion of the year, it was used in recipes of all sorts. Buttermilk is the leftover liquid that drains off the creamy, buttery solids in the process of making butter. Since all milk used for butter making was traditionally unpasteurized, and prepared in non-sterile environments (not necessarily unhygienic environments, however), it would have always been alive with a range of bacteria.

In other words, the traditional form of buttermilk in Wales was a lightly fermented milk drink, not dissimilar in taste to the now popular kefir, skyr and yoghurt. The gut health benefits of these fermented milk drinks have been rediscovered in recent years, leading to a boom in sales and in dairy farmers turning to their production as a means of diversification. Modern supermarket buttermilk – the only form of buttermilk widely available today, even in Wales – isn't at all the same, made as it is using skimmed milk in an industrial process with added cultures, salt sugars and stabilisers. There is sadly no connection at all between this supermarket product and real butter, other than the name. In traditional buttermilk by contrast, the bacteria in the milk and in the surrounding environment would lightly ferment the cream, sometimes even before the butter could be made, creating a milky drink with a slightly sour flavour.

It's impossible to know how ancient a lineage fermented *llaeth enwyn* has as a drink in Wales, but its sour flavour is remarked upon in some of the earliest uses of the term in the Welsh language, including two Elizabethan references to *enwyn llwydsur*, the drinking of sour, grey buttermilk.

The health benefits of traditional buttermilk were, it appears, widely appreciated in the culture historically. One summertime snack enjoyed when the buttermilk was at its best, *bara llaeth enwyn* (bread in buttermilk), was prepared with toasted slices of barley bread that would then be crushed into crumbs and steeped in fresh buttermilk in bowls. This dish was widely held to hold all sorts of medicinal qualities and was claimed to be a cure for tuberculosis.[3]

Perhaps as a result of this esteem for the fermented drink's benefits, Welsh cuisine had further twists on buttermilk drinks, where it was combined with alcoholic drinks or cereals to form refreshing beverages enjoyed at different times of year. *Posel* was the name for a whole grouping of such drinks, where warm buttermilk was curdled using beer or wine with added ingredients to taste, including spices, herbs or treacle (this is similar to the English, Scottish and Dutch 'posset', but with the difference that the drinks known by this name in those countries were usually made with milk, rather than buttermilk). This was both consumed as a beverage and also widely used as a medicine. A Welsh book of medicine in 1740 mentions mint *Posel* as being beneficial 'to relieve or prevent fainting and vomiting', for instance. Similarly, a 1757 letter from a patient to his brother explains how he had 'a sad defluxion on my lungs ... and intend to take *Posel triog* (treacle *Posel*) from the red cup tonight'. Quite apart from the real medical effects of the drink for specific ailments, it was clearly held to be salubrious – and from a gut health point of view, we now know that the bacterial cultures will indeed have contributed to good digestion, at the very least.

Another fermented dish using buttermilk that was still consumed within living memory in rural districts of Wales was *llymru*, from which we have the English word 'flummery'. Here a large quantity of oatmeal was covered with a mix of water and buttermilk and left to stand for some nights until it had turned sour due to the fermentation process. The water was then poured off, the mixture strained and some fresh water added. This mixture was then brought to the boil in a pan, whilst being stirred continuously. In order to test consistency, you would hold the wooden stick a few inches above the saucepan, and if the mixture formed a thin 'tail' as it ran back into the pan, you knew it was ready. It was a common breakfast or supper dish during the summer months, and was also regarded as having medicinal properties.[4]

Llymru and other drinks or dishes like it (including *siot* and *llith*, both also involving oatmeal with buttermilk prepared slightly differently) were universally enjoyed and reviled in equal measure throughout Wales until the mid-20th century. For some they had positive connotations as refreshing summertime and harvest dishes, eaten and enjoyed as refreshing snacks out in the fields during the longer, warmer days. For others however, they were the foods of poverty – one of those dishes that remained available even in the leanest of years – and so acquired the taint of those hard times.[5] This is recorded in countless ditties and rhymes:

> Llymru lled amrwd
> I lenwi bol yn lle bwyd
>
> (Just crude llymru
> That fills the belly instead of food)

Perhaps because of this taint, llymru didn't survive the transition to the commodified food culture of today's Wales. More surprising, given that most of the population of rural Wales born before, say, 1960, remember traditional buttermilk as a normal ingredient in cooking and indeed as a common drink, is how this also disappeared. Like so many of the other foods and dishes in this book, a number of converging factors led to this change, but prime among them was the move away from food production at home to dependence on shops (and increasingly larger chains) for food. It is telling that even Tŷ Tanglwyst doesn't sell buttermilk locally, despite the volume of butter produced on the farm: there is no longer a market for it. Would recreating a demand for buttermilk and some of the old buttermilk dishes in Wales be desirable? In light of the quantities of butter produced and consumed in the country (and the recent rediscovery of the fact that butter beats margarine on health grounds as well as taste) and the health benefits of traditional buttermilk, it would seem so. But as the Parrys and Andy in Llanidloes recognize, recreating a local supply chain for a local product is much harder work than letting mass-market forces destroy one.

Apart from its many uses as a drink, buttermilk was also used alongside butter in making many of the bakestone cakes and breads that were such a distinctive part of Welsh cuisine. Welsh cakes are now the only well-known survivors of this long, mainstream tradition of bakestone baking in Wales but historically they were only one of a great variety of bakestone cakes in Wales. Bakestone and griddles (Welsh: *gradell* or *maen*) are the evolutionary end-point of prehistoric forms of baking on a hearth stone. Although supplanted by ovens in most parts of Europe, bakestone baking survived in some of the north-western fringes of the continent, including Wales and Ireland, and became a sophisticated form of bread- and cake-making that required much skill. Bakestones and iron griddles continued to be used as late as the early eighteenth century by all sections of Welsh society, and are found during this period in the inventories of landed gentry and small, peasant farmers alike.[6] Amongst small farmers and labouring families they remained in constant use throughout the country well beyond this time, and particularly so in more western, rural parts where they continued to be essential kitchen implements well into the 20th century.

Unlike an oven, where the heat builds inside the oven casing and envelops the bread, on a bakestone there is a marked temperature gradient between the hot stone and the cooler air, open to the room circulating around the bread. Different fuels burnt differently – peat, gorse, wood, coal – and the baker (usually the skilled housewife) needed to know how to manipulate them to produce an even heat. There were different ways of gauging whether the right temperature had been reached: 'You'd brush it clean to start with, and take a pinch of oatmeal and spread it across the griddle. If it started to change colour, it was ready. It was hot enough.'[7]

Preparing oatcakes, which were traditionally as important as bread in many parts of Wales, were the most important use for bakestones. Oatcakes were a staple food for many, prepared with oatmeal, a little water and some butter or lard. Other flatbreads were commonly prepared too – *cacen radell* (griddle cake), *cacen soda* (soda cake), *bara crai* (unleavened bread), as well as a range of different pancakes – *crempog furum* (yeast pancakes), *crempog surgeirch* (sour-oat pancakes), *leicecs* (comparable to drop scones) and *slapan* (batter cake).[8] Some of these were sweet tea-time treats, while others were workhorses made to fuel heavy physical labour on the farm or in the mines. The uniting factor of all these griddle cakes is that they were comparatively quick to make and economical in fuel use; it isn't fanciful to link this to the traditionally scattered nature of Welsh settlements, and the culture of dropping by of an evening for music or storytelling by the fire. Upon the visitor's arrival the bakestone could quickly be whisked out and the baked goods served while still warm – with plenty of butter.

Older generations today still corroborate the numerous accounts from all corners of the country of how pancakes and griddle cakes in their various manifestations would always be piled on top of each other and generously lathered with butter so that the butter would ooze down through the pile. This was the favourite comfort food of David Lloyd-George, the wartime British prime minister from Eifionydd in north-west Wales, who would request them every time without fail after coming in from a walk in the cold and wet at his family home near Llanystumdwy. As his housekeeper, Mrs Blodwen Evans, recalled, the cakes would be plastered 'with the lovely salty Welsh butter until they were absolutely soaking with it, and [would be piled high] on a plate – oh how he used to enjoy that!' It was also customary in many areas to prepare a small batch of leavened bread each week on the bakestone, and it was from adding extra lard or butter with currants and sugar to these that Welsh cakes as we know them originated, as a treat for visitors.[9]

The first recorded instance of *teisen gri*, the northern word for Welsh cakes, occurred in 1815 according to the standard Welsh dictionary, although they were undoubtedly made in some form for centuries before this. By the late 19th century, Welsh cakes were well known throughout the country, and had become a popular teatime sweet. Because they could fit easily into coat pockets or small lunch packs, they were often taken to school by children and down mine-shafts by coal miners. By the mid-20th century, with the bakestone tradition dying out at home, Welsh cakes became a speciality of the many covered town markets throughout Wales, where they continue to be made by hand, fresh every day. Even as the other bakestone cakes gradually faded out of popularity over the course of the latter decades of the 20th century, Welsh cakes went from strength to strength, and are now found in supermarkets and corner shops all over the country and beyond.

Wherever they are made, Welsh cakes should be eaten warm from the griddle, always spread with a generous extra dollop of butter on top, and when I return home from Tŷ Tanglwyst that day, I serve up a fresh one from the market lathered with Tŷ Tanglwyst butter. This is comfort food, there's no doubt about it, but unlike a mass-produced chocolate bar or doughnut, this piece of fatty, salty, sugary goodness has roots that extend through bakestones and butter making down to the Welsh lowland meadows grazed by the Loughers' cows and their forebears. It strikes me that the former inhabitants of the hill fort in Tŷ Tanglwyst woods, who would have kept their cows in the fields below, would almost certainly also have been baking on griddles on their hearths. Would they have made buttery cakes on those griddles, perhaps sweetened with honey? It's hard to believe they didn't.

'*Gwŷr a aeth Gatraeth oedd ffraeth eu llu, glasfedd eu hancwyn, a gwenwyn fu ...*'

'The men that went to Catterick were a swift host; fresh mead was their feast, and their poison too ...'

Aneirin, Y Gododdin, 7th century

7

SEIDIR / CIDER

The summons go out across the territories of the Old North. Three hundred of the bravest warriors respond and gather together at *Din Eidyn*, modern-day Edinburgh. There they feast and drink for an entire year. The mead flows and flows, and the testosterone-fuelled crew brags and boasts of the daring exploits to come on the battlefield. But the mead lies to them:

> *Dygymyrrws eu hoet eu hanyanawr*
> *Med evynt melyn melys maglawr*
> *Blwydyn bu llewyn llawer kerdawr*

> [Their high spirits lessened their life-spans.
> They drank mead, gold and sweet, ensnaring;
> For a year the minstrels were merry …]

For when they set out, a dazzling crew celebrated in song, little do they know that on the field of battle they would encounter a force many times their size, and that none save two would live to tell the tale: Cynog, the warrior, and the bard himself. Thus begins what is commonly regarded as the oldest Welsh poem in existence, and one of the earliest pieces of literature native to Britain. The poem recounts how the soldiers of the Welsh kingdom of Manaw Gododdin, located in today's southern Scotland, went to fight a battle at Catterick in modern-day Yorkshire. They did so under the influence of *glasfedd*, mead, which as the poet intimates time and time again, led to their slaughter.

The Welsh taste for mead and other sweet, fruity alcoholic drinks has long been acknowledged, sometimes celebrated, often bemoaned. At the time that the manuscript of this poem was written in the mid-13th century, the events the poem describes already lay six hundred years in the past, but the mead tradition that is so central to the poem's tragedy was still a familiar part of life in Wales. The Welsh mead tradition is by no means unique; mead features in Old Irish, Saxon and Norse poetry, and many eastern European cultures in particular retained a mead-making tradition into modern times. In most parts of western Europe, mead lost out to wine and faded from use during the medieval period. In Wales however, the mead-making tradition survived through the Middle Ages and was then replaced by other native honey-drinks, *meddyglyn* and *bragod*, that only died out during the nineteenth century. When they also eventually disappeared, another sweet (well, sweet, bitter, sharp and more depending on the maker) drink long since produced in Wales and embedded in the culture took their place: cider. And despite the fact that these four drinks are at base different: mead and *meddyglyn* (historically anglicized to metheglin) being fermented honey beverages; *bragod* being at base a form of beer, and cider, of course, being the fermented juice of apples, there is a common thread that unites them all. They are all notably sweet and fruity alcoholic drinks.

We can follow this golden thread by telling the tale of Welsh cider, past and present, as the most resilient of the four beverages.

The word 'cider' earns an appearance in the very first Welsh dictionary, published by the humanist scholar William Salesbury in 1547. The entry simply states '*seidyr* – drink made from cider apples'.[1] But cider had been known and made in Wales for centuries before the word found its way into Salesbury's dictionary. One of the earliest mentions of cider in the British Isles comes, in fact, from the Welsh borderlands, an area that has remained a cider heartland for the best part of a thousand years: the records of the vicarage of Aluredston near Chepstow mention four casks of cider being produced from its orchard in 1286.

Cider is now thought of as an alcoholic drink, but the origins of the word in Old French were far more general. 'Sidre' encompassed any drink made from a variety of wild fruit, but gradually came to denote a drink made primarily from apples, and passed with this meaning into both English and Welsh.[2] The European origins of the cider tradition, in this sense of a drink made exclusively from apples, seem to lie in the Basque Country in the 12th century. From there, the craft of making it spread northwards into Normandy and then up into England and Wales. The first specific reference to cider in England appears in the first decade of the 13th century, when we are told that a certain Robert de Evermore, Lord of Stokesley, paid part of the rent for his properties in Norfolk in 'wine of permain', permain being a type of apple.

The earliest definite reference to cider in the Welsh language appears in a poem which probably dates from the second half of the 14th century. Cider making had spread to nearby Herefordshire by the 14th century, and it seems likely that the practice would have extended from there into the Welsh border countries very rapidly. There were close economic links between Hereford and Wales at the time, and large parts of western Herefordshire were in fact

Welsh-speaking. The close links between that county and Wales – a constant toing and froing of drovers, harvesters, traders, and labourers in both directions – continued for centuries, and one could justifiably claim that cider making in Wales and Herefordshire were essentially two outgrowths of the same tradition, the customs and practices either side of Offa's Dyke being closely reflected on the other.

In Wales, cider became a part of the court culture, with its strong poetic tradition of praise and hospitality. Literary references to cider-drinking are to be found in the poetry of many of the great court poets of the 15th century, with their evocative names: Guto'r Glyn, Gutun Owain, Ieuan Deulwyn. The role of these professional poets was to praise the lavish hospitality, the rich food and delectable drink at their patron's table. Gutun Owain, for example, in his poem of praise to the Abbot Siôn of Valle Crucis Abbey near Llangollen writes:

Dir i mi gan seidr a medd
Oedi gwin a da Gwynedd

(It is not surprising that I, in view of the abundance of cider and mead [at the abbey] do tarry from tasting the wine and bounty of Gwynedd [the next kingdom over])

Here cider and mead are drunk together, and are enough to keep the poet from travelling on and enjoying the wine on offer at the next court on his circuit. Clearly, the native drinks were preferred to French imports by some, at least, during this period.

Orcharding and bee-keeping were well-established practices in all parts of the country by this point, and there is reason to believe that they were not only restricted to the upper classes. We get a tantalizing glimpse into the world of the townsfolk of 14th century Wales in local records from St Asaph in the north-east of the country, where we learn that one of the two orchards within the town's boundaries was owned by two women, called Gwenllian and Tanglwyst.[3] One of the great difficulties in studying the lives of ordinary people during these periods is the paucity of records, but we can take glimpses like this as representing perhaps the tip of an iceberg of town orchards, and perhaps rural ones too. At any rate, cider making was becoming well-established in the south-eastern corner of Wales by the 16th century, in an area centred on Monmouthshire, where the rain shadow cast by the peaks of the Brecon Beacons and the Glamorgan hills offered a warmer, more sheltered climate for fruit growing. In time, Monmouthshire gained great fame for the quality of its produce. The great houses and wealthy farmhouses of the county acquired cider cellars and cider mills from the 16th century onwards, as cider became an important part of the local economy.[4] David Thomas's aforementioned topographical poem published in 1750 describing the main characteristics of the thirteen Welsh counties says of Monmouthshire:

> Gwaith y merched hyn yn union
> Nyddu rhai gwlanenni meinion
> Trin seidr o'r perllannau tewfrith
> A gweithio hetiau gwellt y gwenith

> 'the women here are employed
> In spinning fine flannels
> In making cider from the bounteous orchards
> And in making hats from wheaten straw'

Indeed, cider had become an important selling-point for Monmouthshire taverns by the beginning of the 18th century, as the inscription above the door at the Green House Inn, Llantarnam, testifies: 'Good beer/and Cider for you/come inside/and you may taste it.'

Cider was also known and produced outside these traditional cider-making areas of south-east Wales. The papers of the Mostyn estates in north-east Wales, for example, refer to the widespread growing of apples, apparently for cider making. Records also reveal that in 1673, the good ship 'Margaret' of Westbury in Gloucestershire brought a cargo of 37 hogsheads of cider and perry to Pwllheli in the northwest. From south-west Wales, we learn from John Lewis of Pembroke c.1700 that he had, 'lived to see extensive groves and orchards of my own planting, and from the produce of the latter, have for some years past made a considerable store of cyder annually although my situation be open to the sea'.

More detailed descriptions of the workings of the local cider industry were made at the beginning of the 19th century. Charles Hassell in a publication describing Monmouthshire published in 1813 notes that 'there are orchards in all the vale parts of the county, and some farmers make more cider in plentiful years than their forefathers consume'. Similarly, Walter Davies in his 1815 agricultural survey of south Wales writes of Brecknockshire and Radnorshire, 'the orchards which are planted thrive very well and produce cyder of a good quality both in flavour and strength'.

Despite this, it seems that, on the whole, comparatively little attention was given on most Welsh farms to received opinion as to the best ways of following the art or science of cider making. The aim was simply to produce a large enough quantity of cider for the use of the family and the farm labourers, following the methods with which the family were familiar. Welsh cider, as would have been true of all traditional ciders, would have varied from farm to farm and from year to year, depending on which varieties were planted, the weather and slightly different methods employed. In all cases the resultant liquor, with its quirky, funky notes was not surprisingly quite different in flavour to the supermarket cider available today but was much preferred by its devotees to that more refined, commercial product. Farmhouse cider was generally very dry, completely still, and more importantly, a thirst-quenching, mouth-cleansing drink, which was exactly what was required by those involved in agricultural work. It was also a safe drink, an important consideration in the days of an unreliable water supply. Not only that, but it was also safe from the point of view of strength, as most farmers diluted their cider with water so that its alcohol content ranged between 4.5% and 5.5% – enough to enjoy, but not so much as to impede the ability to work.

The apples were picked from September onwards, and those that had not fallen off the trees were shaken off using an apple hook or 'panking pole'. After picking they were collected into heaps and usually left in the corner of the orchard until required. Popular opinion in both Wales and Herefordshire was opposed to the storing of cider apples indoors on the grounds that this would cause the fruit to dry and not 'run' properly when crushed, even though this was standard practice in other cider making areas. It was also held that a little frost was beneficial as it helped mellow the apples, thereby making them easier to crush. A widely quoted test was that the apples were ready for crushing when they were soft enough for the thumb to be pushed into them perhaps reflecting a folk appreciation of microbial action starting in the fruit, as is also the case with natural wines. But cider makers all had their own opinions on these matters. Some farmers claimed that slightly bruised apples were preferable for cider making. Others separated the apples of different varieties (which ripen and go off at different times) in order to make different tasting ciders. Many Welsh farmers would wait for a convenient point in late autumn when most of the apples were ready and would then throw the whole lot in together and make their cider all at once.[5]

When the apples had ripened enough, it was time to extract the juice which formed the basis of the cider. This was done in two stages; first the fruit had to be broken up or crushed to form a pulp or pomace which was then pressed to extract the juice. The simplest method was to fill a large wooden tub with apples which would then be crushed with a heavy wooden pole, as with a pestle and mortar. This method continued to be used on some Welsh farms into the early twentieth century.[6] Another manual method was by using the dug-out trough cider-mill, which consisted of a hollowed log in which apples were placed. A heavy stone was then rolled back and forth in the trough thereby crushing the apples.

It was, however, the stone cider mill, first introduced in the seventeenth century, which was most commonly used for crushing apples. An example mill is also preserved at the St Fagans museum; it is a circular structure roughly seven feet in diameter with a rubble base on top of which is set a trough or 'chase' of stone. An upright stone is run along this trough, which is connected by an axle to a wooden framework in such a way that a horse or donkey can be harnessed; as the animal walks around the mill the apples are crushed. Water was poured into the trough at intervals to prevent the crushed apples from sticking to the roller; the most commonly favoured source of this water on Welsh farms was the duck pond. Crushing was slow work and was normally kept for those days when outside work on the farm was impossible due to bad weather – a not infrequent phenomenon in late autumn in Wales. Little more than half a ton of apples could be crushed in a day using this method.

The earliest known stone mill of this kind in Wales is dated

1770 and was found at Craig-y-bwla farm near Crickhowell, but the existence of a number of seventeenth-century cider-mill houses suggests that the method is much older. At the beginning of the 1980s, it was estimated that 150 stone cider mills of this type survived in the cider-making areas of Wales, though very few were still in use. As the nineteenth century progressed, another option became available to farmers: the travelling cider maker. These itinerant makers went from farm to farm with a portable cider mill and had their heyday during the first half of the twentieth century. A typical example was Mr C. T. Morris of Raglan who began making cider in 1928, visiting 40 farms on his round, and who by 1946 was visiting 67 different farms each year. They enabled smaller farmers without the means to build a stone cider mill to make their own cider on their farm. The volume of cider produced by one of these mills in a year was not insubstantial – 18,000 gallons – but this declined significantly during the 1950s as demand dropped so that in 1959, his final year, he produced a mere 180 gallons. The visit of the cider maker was a social event in these areas, and it was a custom for neighbouring farmers to assemble in a particular farm on a Sunday morning to gossip and taste 'the quality of the year's cider'.'

The second step, after crushing, was pressing the pomace. At one time heavy oak presses were used, but these were replaced during the nineteenth century by lighter presses with iron fittings. Because pomace was so runny it had to be held in some way to be pressed; in the west of England, it was mixed with alternate layers of straw for this purpose, but in Wales farmers preferred to use 'hairs'. These were large, coarse mats made from horse-hair. They held the pomace in place while allowing the liquid to flow out. The pomace was laid out on the first 'hair', and several hairs were then built up in this way to form what was known as a 'cheese'.

The beam was then screwed down onto the cheese slowly, exerting maximum pressure, and if possible the press was left screwed down overnight, because the last runnings from the cheese were considered a particular delicacy. The apple juice which flowed out of the cheese was then collected in a shallow tub placed at the base of the press. The dried pomace which remained after the pressing was used as animal feed, and there are several cautionary tales concerning this practice – not only might animals become drunk on it, but the laxative properties of the pomace made it extremely perilous for anyone to venture too close to the rear quarters of animals fed in this way. In earlier times, pomace was also used as a soil fertilizer or mixed with coal and put on the back of the fire as fuel.

After pressing, the apple juice was transferred to wooden casks for fermentation and storage. Up to this point cider making is a simple mechanical operation: it's from here onwards that the mysterious parts of the process begin. Yeasts which occur naturally in the air (and not on the skins of the apples, as was commonly believed by farmers) are responsible for this process, and most farmers would let them do their work on the juice without interference. A few would occasionally 'feed' the yeast by adding sugar, beetroot or even meat. No trace of this food would be left at the end of the fermentation process, adding to its mystery. Fermentation usually lasted between two and four weeks, unless the weather was particularly cold. Once it was over the barrels were sealed and left for three or more months (the cider remained in a stable, drinkable condition for up to five years) before it was drunk.

Everyone – other than members of the temperance movements – drank this cider, but farm labourers above all. Cider was an important part of their salary, and this custom continued even after its prohibition by law in 1887. 'No cider, no work' was the axiom often heard, and it was hard for farmers who had a reputation for poor cider to attract and retain workers. Between two and four quarts a day appears to have been the customary allowance in Wales, and labourers often carried their cider to the fields in small wooden costrels which held about half a gallon each. Cider was drunk at all times of the day and year, and it was customary to offer a glass of cider to any visitor who came to the farm. Not everyone approved of the situation however. The availability of cider was considered to lead to cases of drunkenness, accidents and brawls. In the 1847 report on education in Wales (notoriously known as the report of the 'Blue Books'), part of the section on Brecknock reads: 'the morals of the Country are certainly very defective, owing to the system of drinking cider etc., so prevalent here: drunkenness is the common sin of both farmer and their servants ... in harvest time this practice is still more prevalent'.

After the Second World War great changes took place in all branches of agriculture and in most of Europe, and it is fair to argue that the rapid decline of farm cider production was only one part of the wider move away from self-sufficient mixed farms towards an economy dominated by large commercial producers. One important factor was the large decrease in the numbers of farm labourers, which led to a large drop in the demand for cider on farms. People's tastes in drink changed too, as cheap, sugary cider from large factories came on to the market, less labour-intensive farm work meant there was less need for a thirst-quenching drink and orchards became less valuable in a monetary economy; apples were not a cash crop for most farmers. A few farmers persisted into the 1960s and 1970s, but the main stream of this tradition which had united the counties of south-east Wales in their love of the drink of the apple tree seemed to have come to an end.

Llanblethian Orchards

Alex Simmens was a student in Cardiff in the early 2000s, and a member of the student Real Ale society in the city. One day he found himself being asked to manage the cider bar at a festival in the city and got into traditionally made ciders – a far cry from the mass-produced commercial ciders made with industrial yeasts and added sugars usually found in UK supermarkets. He started touring cider farms in south Wales and beyond, visiting cider makers and helping to pick apples at harvest time. Through serendipity (and the small size of the cider scene in Wales at the time) he met Dave and Fiona Matthews, who, at that time, ran a small cidermaking business called 'Seidr Dai' – 'Dai' being the familiar form of Dafydd, the Welsh for David.

By this point, despite a few new faces trying to start a revival in Welsh cider making in the 1980s and 1990s, there were really only a handful of farms left in Monmouthshire still producing cider from their own apples in the old tradition – and fewer still that were selling any. But thanks to the happy coincidence of two unrelated events, the early 2000s saw a small renaissance in Welsh cider making. The first of these events was the formation of the Welsh Perry and Cider society in 2001, by Dave Matthews, Alan Golding and others. 'It started off as effectively a group of cider-lovers – and cidermakers – sitting in the Clytha Arms and talking about how to revitalise cider making,' explains Alex. The Clytha Arms, a village pub in rural Monmouthshire in the heart of the old cider-making country, was as near a cider heartland as still existed in Wales at the time. They ran a Welsh cider and Perry festival – which is still going strong – and it grew from there.

The second event, entirely unrelated, was that the large Herefordshire cidermaker, Bulmers, having been bought out by a multinational corporation, cancelled a number of its contracts all at once that year. Many Monmouthshire farmers that had long supplied them with fruit found themselves with a surplus of fruit – and cider apples at that. 'And so a lot of them decided to just make some themselves. Their fathers had made cider, many of them, and in many cases there was still a cidermill and cider press either on their farm or at a neighbour's.'

And so Alex entered the scene at a fortuitous moment. He started making cider in his parents' house using a handmade wooden press and a mix of eating and cooking apples scrounged from family and friends. Then in 2006, he started planting apple trees on land the family owned in the village of Llanblethian on the outskirts of Cowbridge. 'I was pretty much making it up as I went along at this point, to be honest,' he recounts, 'although I'd been with cidermakers, and was really into cider, I didn't have any practical knowledge of growing trees, nor any realisation of the sheer differences between apple varieties, and the massive effect that has on the cider you make. So I just planted a huge range of varieties, and hoped that some would do well. But I did feel that having such a range of varieties would help me learn about the varieties, and spread the risk for the future – which it has.'

Over the next three winters they planted 120 apple and perry pear trees on the land, which I visit on a warm September day, with the bulging fruit sparkling in the rays of the lowering autumn sun. The site is quite a suntrap, nine acres of valley bottom between two tree-covered slopes in the fertile and mild Vale of Glamorgan. The (apple) news and cybersphere is full of reports this September of a poor harvest with crops decimated in the main English fruit-growing regions due to late frosts and bad weather. Here, it's been a good year in what is one of the sunniest parts of Britain, only a couple of miles from the sea's moderating influence. The trees are heavy with crops of umpteen apple varieties and half as many pear varieties; as I arrive, Alex has four tubs full of pears. 'This is the last half hour's haul,' he says, gesturing at the golden, round pears, 'and I need to fill this trailer by the end of the afternoon.'

Only two and a half acres of the nine on the site are down to orchard. The rest is intentionally left as a mixture of scrub, regenerating natural woodland and wetland. The grass and undergrowth on most of the site is cut once a year, to enable it to carry wildflowers for as much of the year as possible to encourage insect life and wildlife more generally. Having been in the family a long time, the site has never been sprayed, as Alex explains. 'We have grass-snakes, and herons, egrets – all sorts of birds. A huge variety of wildflowers, watermint and watercress in the ditches … And because we don't spray the fruit-trees at all, either, we have a lot of insects. The only downside is that when we get diseased trees – which does happen, not least because some of the varieties I planted turn out not to be so suitable for this climate – they need to go to stop it spreading. But that's ok – I can graft them over with a different variety, mostly.'

'We don't fertilise at all, no manure, nothing. There's no need,' Alex explains. The valley of the river Thaw is, despite its now gentle appearance, an old glacial valley with heavy grey clay underneath. A foot of topsoil – all floodplain – underneath which lie at least two metres of grey clay, and then alluvial layers and grit; so no bedrock whatsoever. But the clay is fertile – they've never had an issue with too little nitrogen in the fruit, or with hydrogen sulphite (i.e. rotten egg smell), which could occur were the yeast struggling during fermentation due to lack of nutrients in the fruit. But clay in a floodplain can also be wet, and slow to warm up. The response, drawing on the old tradition of cider making on the low-lying Gwent levels twenty miles to the east, was to plant the trees on raised mounds.

'I think because of that the trees should be fine if the land does flood, but we've never actually had a flood here. That might partly be because of the fact that we've left the trees and the scrub, that we've got the watercress and the other water plants in the rills – it all slows the water down, doesn't it?' Alex says, as he shows me some of the water channels that criss-cross the land, with the lazy sound of water insects buzzing gently around us. He remembers some of the local men coming to harvest the watercress with a hook when he was a boy, continuing a Glamorgan tradition that the 18th century antiquarian Iolo Morganwg describes as peculiar to the country people in that part of Wales in his day.

I ask Alex about cidermaking, and in what sense he sees himself as standing in the long Welsh cider-making tradition. 'Well, I learnt so much of what I know from Dave Matthews; and he had picked all sorts of things up from and knew personally that older generation of Monmouthshire farmers who remembered the old farmhouse cidermaking ways – so that's one thing', he says pensively. 'And in many ways, the orchard here is very similar to the orchards that farms would have had around here up to the Second World War. We have large, standard trees – not those bush trees in rows that commercial orchards have these days – and we harvest the fruit by hand with a panking pole.' Alex's is a modern, home-made one. 'And of course, having the trees planted on mounds, and not spraying the land – all of that is very much the way things were done tradition-ally. But the main thing it comes down to really is the varieties', he finishes. I ask him to explain further, and we set off for a walk around the orchard.

'There are 36 different apple varieties here, and 16 perry pear varieties. With cider you're looking for a range of different flavours, so some varieties are sharps, some sweets, others bittersharp, others bittersweet. That's how the Long Ashton research station in Somerset differentiated them, and it's a good way to classify cider apples. And then you can add sweet dessert apples to the mix to add a bit more sugar to your cider. The Swedish variety "Katy" is one of those', he says, indicating a tree with luscious, bright red fruit, which when I bite into it floods my mouth immediately with juice. 'I also have some classic English cider varieties growing here, like a few trees of "Dabinett", which is a bittersweet, or "Sweet Coppin", which is a sweet. They're good because they give a bit of backbone to your cider, and are quite dependable.'

'But one of my absolute favourites is over here.' He takes me to a cluster of trees that all bear the same burgundy red apple with a little scarf skin. 'This is Frederick – one of the Welsh varieties. A real vintage variety – so useful in cidermaking.' Frederick is a Victorian variety, widely grown in Monmouthshire historically, although originating in the Forest of Dean. It raises the question as to what a 'Welsh variety of apple' is, particularly when it comes to borderland areas around Monmouthshire, where the border moved through the centuries, and where Welsh was spoken until the early 19th century in neighbouring parts of Herefordshire. The working definition at the National Botanic Garden of Wales seems to be any variety that was either first raised in Wales, or that was widely cultivated in the country historically. But even taking the tighter definition of only those apples originally raised in Wales, there are almost forty Welsh apple cultivars.

Alex is growing a number of them; Cummy Norman, Pig Aderyn, Breakwell's Seedling, Pen Caled, all of which bring out different notes in the cider. The latter of these, for instance, makes a dry but fragrant and fruity champagne-like beverage, with a hint of pear drops. Alex has his own favourites to work with; 'I really rate Breakwell's' (originating near Monmouth) 'and Pig Aderyn' (from St Dogmaels, Pembrokeshire) – 'they're very good cider varieties, both of them sharp/bittersharp. Pig Aderyn is very juicy too. That seems to be how the Welsh liked their ciders, judging from the varieties that have survived – quite acidic, more on the fruity side of things, rather than high tannins and bitter notes you get in Somerset, for instance. In fact, in the early twentieth-century, the bigger Herefordshire cider companies used to routinely add sugar to their cider before coming over to sell it in Wales. The drinking public just wanted a sweeter, fruitier, lighter product than people the other side of Offa's Dyke.'

I reflect on this over a pint of Alex's 'Breakwell' cider many months later. Most ciders are made with a blend of varieties, and within the cider world only a few classic varieties are regarded as being rounded enough to create convincing single-variety draughts. So I am amazed, in the most pleasantly possible way, when I swill the first mouthful and discover the most honeyed, smooth and refreshing cider I have possibly ever tasted. I am drinking with my mother, and we both try to put our finger on the green apple flavour coming through, and then we've got it; of course, it's apple crumble: fruity, light and gently sweet. The sort of flavour that takes you to the end of a long summer day's harvesting – even if you've never done that sort of work yourself.

Gwin, meddyglyn, bragod, bir
This brings me full circle, linking the long-standing farm cider tradition, expressed most prominently in the native varieties developed

for cider making in this country, with the old mead and bragod traditions. Particularly given the strong links between the coastal counties of Wales and the counties of south-western England – with trade passing back and forth across what the Welsh called the Severn Sea (*Môr Hafren*) and the English the Bristol channel – the difference between the fruity Welsh cider apples and the tanniny apples and ciders of Somerset is striking. When this is coupled with the survival of honey-drinks in the form of mead, *meddyglyn* and *bragod*, it seems indisputable that Welsh drinking culture has had a long-standing preference for sweeter and fruitier alcoholic drinks.

Those now lost honey-drinks are themselves fascinating examples of the development of a home-grown tradition over many centuries. *Meddyglyn* ('Metheglin') was for a time almost ubiquitous in Wales, with the first references appearing as early as the 13th century. The visiting Nathaniel Crouch mentions it in his description of the people's diet in Flintshire in 1695; 'of milk, butter, cheese and honey there is plenty; of the last of which they make great quantities of a drink like Muscadine, call'd Metheglin', and it continued in common use into the early years of the 19th century. This was a form of mead with herbs and sometimes spices added, that was widely regarded as having strong medicinal properties as an elixir or tonic, and it continued to be made and enjoyed long after pure mead had fallen out of fashion. The famous physicians of Myddfai in Carmarthenshire, who collected copious notes on herbal remedies in Wales, prescribed *meddyglyn* for all manner of illnesses. It was still being produced in a diluted form in the mid-19th century in Ceredigion, when the recipe required a gallon of water to be added to the large amount of honey, and hops were the herb added for flavour. This was made in June, and stored in large earthenware jars that would be buried in boggy land until the following spring.

Bragod (braggot) has as long a pedigree in Wales, despite never catching on in other countries. Like many good tipples, the basic idea is startlingly simple: mixing mead with beer, sometimes with the addition of spices. For palates accustomed to dark, bitter ales this is undoubtedly a travesty, but within a drinking culture awash with mead and fruity cider, this was a natural option to develop to complete the range. *Bragod* is mentioned in the early Welsh laws, in mythology and in medieval poetry. By 1597 we find it alongside the other drinks in an enumeration of the Welsh tipples, confirming the idea that these were the drinks of choice: *Gwin, meddyglyn, bragod, bir / kwrw a sir fwythvsol* (Wine, metheglin, braggot and beer/ale and sumptuous cider). Although brewed throughout the year, it was particularly associated with Easter Monday, a day of jollity and games after the privations of Lent. The young women of the parish would customarily invite all the young men they met on their way to the village for the games to the public house for a drink of *bragod*. Industrialization seems to have also sounded the death knell for *bragod* as a major part of life, with the last mention of it in 1838.[8]

But the preference for sweeter drinks did not only manifest itself in these two twists on honey tipples. Country wines made with hedgerow and forest fruits are widely attested in older recipes – including sloe, damson, elderflower and gorse wine – and also by visitors to Wales such as the traveller Thomas Dineley, who says of his visit to Cardiganshire in 1684; 'They have choice wine also of their own growth off the mountains, which the Welsh Gentlewomen make of Resberryes and which abound in these parts.' One of these in particular was frequently remarked upon by visitors to Wales, namely *diodgriafol*, an alcoholic beverage made using the berries of the mountain ash, or rowan tree. As the name suggests, this tree is more common in upland parts of the country, which are significantly less suited to growing orchard trees. This was the drink of choice for poorer people in these regions. As an observer put it in 1803 when describing the cooking quarters of a poor cottager's family on the Elenydd mountains in mid-Wales, 'a kettle, with a backstone for baking oaten cakes … diod griafol, the usual beverage of the family'. The method of preparation involved steeping rowanberries in boiled water, and then leaving the mixture for a month or so to ferment, at the end of which month the result would be a 'pleasant acid drink'.[9] This was by all accounts enjoyable enough, and called by some at the time berry cider; an 1831 account of the drink compares the flavour favourably to perry.[10]

Between all these drinks, which all sat alongside beer as the drink of choice in Wales for a thousand years and more, there is to all appearances a clear affinity in their sweeter, fruitier flavour. This stands in clear distinction to English, Belgian or Dutch liking for darker, malty or bitter drinks, and is enough of a longstanding tendency to justify the speculation to the effect that the Welsh cider varieties' fruitier tendencies seem to hold a faint echo of the Gododdin's soldiers' fatal penchant for mead. Some food habits seem to die hard.

In an echo of those former farmers who would separate out their different varieties for cidermaking, Alex tells me that the best cidermakers work with the varieties they have. 'You want to bring the variety's own flavours to the fore, not drown it in some blend of everything you've got. You have to treat the varieties differently – and that's as true of the fruit when you're making cider as it is of the tree when you're growing it. And then you have to think carefully about how you're going to make the cider. Are you going to use oak barrels to balance out tannins? With the Welsh cider apples, you want to bring out the fruity aroma, emphasise the lightness of the drink – maybe something like méthode champenoise is appro-priate, adding bubbles to it.' Llanblethian orchards' cider, suffice to say, tends towards single varietals rather than blends, 'though the pubs usually want blends', Alex adds.

I ask him to what extent he can support himself from the cider-making. 'Well, in one sense, we could grow more and so sell more by doing things differently. But it comes down to what I want to make – which is really special, good quality cider – and what people want to buy, which sadly isn't that. Cider has a real image problem. These days people see it as a nice summertime drink, but they just don't realise that real cider is a craft product that is easily compar-able to wine. Just like wine, soil, climate, *terroir*, fruit variety and method all make a massive difference to the end product. Except that with wine, the law places limits on what people can call wine. With cider, you can add all sorts of chemicals, all sorts of flavour-ings to your drink, and still call it cider. In Spain it needs to be 100% apple juice to be called cider. In the UK, that's 35%. So those of us making the real thing suffer massively from that lack of regulation. Even compared to beer, people are not prepared to pay for cider, no matter how many awards it's won or how it's made.' So for Alex as for many cidermakers in Wales, the work is seasonal, supplemented by other work through winter and early spring once the harvest is in and the apples are pressed.

I leave still pondering how it came about that the cider trad-ition in Wales disappeared so absolutely from Welsh culture and consciousness in a way that it never did in the other traditional cidermaking parts of Europe – Asturias, Normandy, Devon, for example. Alex had an explanation that rings true. 'There used to be a pub in Cardiff – it closed decades ago now – called "The Greyhound". It was a proper old cider pub, and back in the day it would have got its cider from Monmouthshire farms. A guide to Cardiff pubs from 1967 complains that the quality of the scrumpy there isn't what it used to be. The place was notorious. It had an awful reputation – you know, brawls, fights, drinking-till-you-black-out sort of place. And that's what people in Wales associated with cider. I think some of that is still there, at some level.' This seems a great shame, particularly in view of the survival of the tradition by the skin of its teeth, and the dozens of native apple varieties to have survived despite the recent decades of neglect.

From the coast just a few miles south of Alex's orchard you can look over to the hills of north Somerset, for English aficionados perhaps the spiritual home of cider with the distinctive local bittersharp tradition. It's true that even English cider, with a greater following and a more active base of drinkers, hasn't yet managed to reassert itself in the national consciousness in a way comparable with either beer or wine. This is a pity: real cider, made only with the fermented juice of freshly pressed apples, is every bit as varied and as subtle a drink as wine. As Alex said, poor regulation has had a part to play in this state of affairs, but public taste is ultimately of greater consequence. If the demand is there, the product will surely come. Does this matter, when all we are talking about is a drink like cider? I think it does: a world without the traditional lightly fruity ciders of Wales, and the long tradition of sweet alcoholic drinks that lie behind them, would be a poorer place. But without a doubt, Wales is a richer place for the survival of this fruity tradition thus far.

Tatws Pum Munud

bacon rashers
potatoes
onions
salt and pepper
a little flour
water

Fry the bacon rashers in a deep frying pan and then
lift onto a plate. Slice the potatoes and onions and fry
in the bacon fat. Season well and sprinkle with a little
flour. Then add water so that the potatoes are barely
covered and lay the bacon rashers on top. Cook
slowly until the water is absorbed and the potatoes
turn golden brown.[11]

8

SGLODION / CHIPS

On the lunchtime I visit, Ferry Cabin has that steady contented buzz you only find in establishments well known and frequented by their customers. Someone pops their head around the door and throws a question to an older man having his cup of tea at the far end of the café. He shouts back a gruff reply. A young woman comes in asking for chips after the 'closed' sign has gone up; 'Can't you read?' jokes Paul, the owner, before filling a carton with chips for her. One of the first things Paul says to me about the café is that 'this is not a fish and chip shop. We're a café – we're not even allowed to enter the "best fish and chips in Britain" award, so how can we be a fish and chip shop?' He's right of course – by definition – but a feature of Welsh food culture, for a century and more, is that a place that does proper fish and chips *is* a sort of 'chippy' in people's heads, whatever else it might also be – restaurant, pub, café or ice-cream van. They have to be *proper* fish and chips, mind – and Ferry Cabin certainly does them properly.

The Carmarthenshire village of Ferryside, of which the 'Cabin', as it's affectionately known, stands at the heart, is named after the ferry that for centuries ploughed across the Tywi estuary to the old

Norman township of Llansteffan on the western shore. After a long hiatus, the ferry is now back in action, primarily serving tourists who come to enjoy the estuarine views, the crag-top castle at Llansteffan, the beach and the gentle green hills of this quiet corner of Wales. At the centre of the village beside the station on the main square sits Ferry Cabin. The first café on the site was housed in a hut, and bore the name 'Enterprise Café'. Val's grandfather opened it. Val was Ferryside's last postmistress, who retired a few years ago, and the village post office with her. Her Grandad, it seems, had opened it with winnings from a bet on a horse in the 1933 Grand National. Opening a new café in Ferryside in the 1930s was indeed enterprising given that at the time there were already six or seven cafés in the village, whose most important clientele were the miners of the western valleys of the south Wales coalfield. They would come down to Ferryside en masse for their summer break; photos from the era show Ferryside's now tranquil one-platform station thronging with suitcases and families on their annual trip to the seaside.

The hut was replaced in time by a solid building, and at some point that became 'Ferry Cabin'. By the 1990s, it was the only café left in the village, and it closed in 2001. On 10 October 2001, Paul and Jean Griffiths of Penrhiwgoch farm, just outside the village, were down in the square looking at the pub opposite, which was for sale. It was taken off the market that day but they saw the Cabin instead – and bought it. 'We worked all the hours God gave those first years', recalls Paul. 'The place was open from eight until eight, six days a week, and we'd just have the Wednesday off to do all the farm work. But we needed to make the place pay, so that's what we had to do, really.' I've come to visit because I want to learn about fish and chips from farm to fork, and I've been told there's nowhere better to learn than here.

Fish and chips is a speciality of the British Isles, a seemingly permanent feature of the food landscape that was actually first established in the 1860s (in London or Lancashire – or both). This may well be by imitation of one of the dishes brought by Sephardi Jews who came from Spain and Portugal to the United Kingdom from the 1650s onwards, and who prepared *pescado frito* (fried fish) using cod to eat on Shabbat. By 1910 there were already over 25,000 fish and chip shops across the UK, and the government prioritized guarding the supply of fish and chips during the First World War to keep morale high. During the twentieth century the dish entered global consciousness as one of the defining 'British' dishes, and early on it became a lynchpin of Welsh food habits, a status it has since retained. There is a chippy in every town, suburb and large village in Wales, almost all family run and many sporting humorous names – 'O! My Cod!', 'A fish called Rhondda' or 'Y Dafarn Datws' (The Potato Pub).

But despite their ubiquity, even the raw material for chips – the humble potato – is a relative newcomer on the scene. It's a native of the Andes, and the first written mention of a potato in Europe is a receipt for delivery to Belgium from 1567. But widespread adoption of the *solanum tuberosum* had to wait until Europeans' initial suspicions had been allayed, and its usefulness as a dependable staple crop widely accepted. From the 1750s onwards, a combination of promotion by government officials and aristocratic landowners, and poor harvests from grains due to the Little Ice Age led to the spread of the potato across the continent amongst the farming and peasant classes. Potatoes had the further advantage over grains of being easy to grow on smaller plots of land, and didn't need to be milled before they were used in cooking. Acceptance and use spread gradually across Europe, with some regions for varying cultural and agricultural reasons quicker to adopt the new tuber than others.

Potatoes were by all accounts in common use by the farming and peasant communities by the end of the 18th century. On his tour of Wales in 1805, E. Donovan writes that 'the common food of the cottager appears to be potatoes, for which a scanty patch or strip of land is considered as a necessary appendage to every little habitation'. But no more than a century earlier, the potato was little known in Wales. The first recorded use of a variant of the word in Welsh outside a dictionary occurs as late as 1765. The picture seems to bear out the wider European pattern of differentiated acceptance by region – Heath Malkin comments in 1804 that, compared to neighbouring Glamorgan, in Brecknockshire 'the gardens and potato grounds are not universal, and seem, where they are possessed, not to be very highly valued'. Five years earlier however, according to Richard Warner they were already an accepted part of the dietary mix in mountainous, isolated Meirionydd: '[the peasant's] diet is not contemptible – oaten cake, or bread made by a mixture of wheat and rye, hard cheese, *potatoes* and excellent butter-milk, furnish a meal substantial and wholesome'.

Unsurprisingly, perhaps, given the later popularity of the dish in the country, potatoes were quickly paired with fish when they arrived in Welsh kitchens with one of the earliest references to potatoes being used in Wales occurring in a gardening and cooking manual published in 1744, *Adam's Luxury and Eve's Cookery*, where it is noted that the Welsh bake 'potatoes with herrings, mixed with layers of pepper, vinegar, salt, sweet herbs and water'.[1] Another widespread recipe combined salted herrings with jacket potatoes. It seems that there were plenty of Welsh precursors to fish and chips.

Despite tropes of Welsh conservatism when it came to new

foods and farming methods, potatoes were adopted with gusto and combined with the existing mainstays of the cuisine – dairy produce, bacon, root vegetables and alliums – to produce new dishes that retained their popularity in rural communities until the late twentieth century. Their functional names belie the mouth-watering realities; *Tatws pum munud* [five-minute potatoes] is a dish of thinly sliced potatoes cooked slowly in a frying pan, with a little water, flour and a layer of bacon; or alternatively added to onions and covered with milk or cream before being cooked in the oven. Or for something richer, *tato pobi* [baked potatoes]; 'potatoes and onions cooked between two layers of bacon in a cauldron.[2] Simmer gently in a little water until the water evaporates and the potato browns in the bacon fat'.[3] *Tatws popty* [roast potatoes] was a dish with variants across north Wales; 'place a thick layer of pota-toes and onions on the bottom of a large meat tin and cover with water. Place the joint on top and roast in a hot oven.'[4] Simpler dishes included the perennially popular *tatws llaeth* – potatoes boiled and then served with buttermilk.

Then there is mash, that combination of potato and dairy par excellence. It is crowned with at least five different names in Welsh – *tato potsh*, *tato pwno*, *tatws stwmp*, *tatws stwnsh*, *tato wedi masho*, before we even get to *tato bwts* for a mixed potato and swede mash or *mwtrin* for a mash including potatoes, swede and peas or car-rots. All these dishes were commonly served with buttermilk.[5] And potatoes also quickly won their place in *cawl*, to such a degree that by the mid-19th century they often comprised much of the dish's calorific value amongst poorer families, with the meat merely add-ing flavour. In lean times a second lot of potatoes were added to the previous day's soup which was reheated to make *cawl eildwym* – 'second-warmth cawl'.

Despite the potato's swiftly won ubiquity, and perhaps significantly for an understanding of the country's food history and its social history alike, Wales was left largely unscathed by the potato famines of the mid-19th century, in contrast to its neighbours in Ireland and Scotland – and indeed other parts of Europe. There were outbreaks of scurvy in the wake of the potato blight in Scotland (1846) and in Ireland and England (1847) – but this seems not to have been the case in Wales. Scurvy is caused by a deficiency of vitamin C in the diet so its presence or absence acts as a good indicator of how varied people's diets are, and particularly their fruit and veg intake. Potatoes can be a source of vitamin C, but it is a measure of the lack of other sources in the diets of the poor in Scotland and Ireland that, by the 1840s, potatoes seem to have become the principal source of vitamin C for many. Data on potato intake in Wales before 1850 show that it was lower than in other parts of the British Isles but higher than in Switzerland, for instance. All of this is consistent with the suggestion that the Welsh had a diet that was sufficiently varied in fresh vegetables (as we shall see in the next chapter) to contain high enough levels of vitamin C throughout the year to withstand scurvy, even with lower potato consumption. Indeed, according to an enquiry into the foods of the working classes conducted in 1863 across the United Kingdom, the labouring classes in Wales were found to be generally better fed than their counterparts in England.[6]

Conditions for potato cultivation are particularly favourable along south-western coastal swathes, where the sea's moderating influence is at its greatest and damaging late frosts in spring are almost unknown. The coastal tips of Pembrokeshire around St David's and Marloes are well known for their earlies, and traditionally would race against Cornwall to have the first potatoes on the market. *Tato newy* – 'Pembrokeshire earlies' are looked forward to every year, and it's fair to say that potatoes remain generally popular in Wales. When the Aldi supermarket chain introduced Welsh-grown potatoes in their 47 Welsh stores in July 2017, sales of potatoes from those stores grew by 33% over the ensuing five months.[7]

One of the uses to which potatoes were put was, of course, making chips. The origin of chips themselves (and the confusion in English between the terms 'chips', 'crisps' and 'French fries') remains highly contested, with various countries including Belgium, France, England and the USA claiming the crown as chips' birthplace. The earliest uncontested record is found in a book called *The Cook's Oracle*, published in 1822 by the American William Kitchiner.[8] This includes a recipe for 'potatoes fried in slices or shavings' which are then served with salt. An 1825 English book featuring much the same recipe calls them 'pommes de terre frites', indicating a French origin to the recipe. Intriguingly however, at an earlier date than both of these a recipe 'to fry potatoe chips' was already circulating among the gentry in northern Wales.

Plas Newydd is one of the most exquisite timber-framed buildings anywhere in the British Isles, built in the early 18th century. It was bought in 1780 by two Irish women, Eleanor Butler and Sarah Ponsonby, who settled there together and became known as the Ladies of Llangollen, entertaining many visitors from high society including Wordsworth, Shelley, Lord Byron and Sir Walter Scott. Amongst their circle of friends was a Mrs Mytton of Oswestry (*Croesoswallt* – long regarded as part of Wales) who in February 1819 sent them a recipe for potato chips.[9] To this she added a reference to a similar method of cooking Jerusalem artichokes at Wynnstay, the home of another neighbour; both potatoes and Jerusalem artichokes were grown in the gardens at Plas Newydd. This recipe recognizably describes the process of making chips, frying them and then serving sprinkled with salt:

> Take raw potatoes. pare the outside – then pare them round or in as long pieces as you can – wash them well in water … remain in it about an hour then put them on a sieve before the fire for about half an hour before you fry them – dust a little flour over them in very hot fat till crisp and of a nice light brown colour – drain them from the fat – and sprinkle a little salt over them – then serve them. I suspect the Jerusalem Artichokes so admired at Wynnstay – were done in the same manner.

The reference to Wynnstay – another stately home in nearby Ruabon – implies that recipes of this sort were circulating among the upper classes in the region at this time, a few years before the recipes published in Kitchiner's cookbook. So while Wales may not be the origin of either chips or fish and chips as a dish, both made an early appearance here.

Origins aside, their status as street food caught on early. One of the first fish and chip shops on record in Wales was opened on Caroline Street in central Cardiff by a Mr Rees and a Mr Hopkins in the 1870s, only a few years after the first one opened in London. It was marketed as selling the cheapest chips in town, implying that other establishments were already selling them. 'As cheap as Caroline Street chips' became a phrase in the city because of the sign in their window reading 'Cheap Skate and Chips, 2d'. Over time, 'Cheap Alley' became 'chip alley', the now long-standing moniker for Caroline Street among Cardiffians. Most of the businesses on the alley today are independent, family-run takeaways, with several fish and chip shops serving 'arf'n'arf' or 'half-and-half', the local speciality of pairing chips and rice. Fish and chip outlets proliferated through the closing years of the 19th century, and by the early 20th century they were found throughout the country.

Today, chips retain their place as the crowning pinnacle of potato intake in the country. Universally loved, they are a comfort food, with 87% of Welsh 10-year-olds eating chips in a four-day period.[10] It is true to say that fish and chips, like the other classic combinations (pie and chips, faggots and chips), are above all a working class dish: tasty, filling, affordable and not too poor on the nutritional scales. In Wales they are dishes of unparalleled social importance that are expected to sit on café, pub and takeaway menus across the country. Viewed from an Irish or English perspective this is thoroughly unremarkable, but viewed on a broader European or Western canvas, the sheer social importance of takeaway chips represents part of a particular food tradition. The best place to get chips in a given area is a piece of local knowledge held in common – and can be elicited from anyone, with an informed opinion behind it in most cases. People congregate in these social institutions. Standing in a queue on a Friday evening (Friday fish very much remains a thing when it comes to fish and chips) and exchanging pleasantries; going out for lunch on the same day to the same café; having a meal down the local pub. These are rituals that continue, and that form reference points within wider society: whatever some may say, it is of these things that food cultures are made.

Back in Ferryside, Paul affirms this, 'it's the regulars that keep us going. I'd say we get 25% of the village in here regularly. They come from Ferryside, from the outer villages – Broadlay, Broadway, Llansaint – and from Kidwelly and beyond. We don't advertise at all, so the tourists we get are a bonus. But it's fun, see? It's the banter and the joking with the locals – you wind people up but actually, you get to know them.'

It's obvious that Paul is himself one of the lynchpins of this social institution. 'I've got the memory of an elephant', he tells me more than once. 'So we get people coming in, they look at the menu and they're like "I can't decide!". So I tell them what they had last time – "you had the steak and Guinness last time". And if they're new they're always amazed and more often than not they'll ask how I know that. "You were on Table 12", I say! But in all seriousness, we have got a lot of regulars, particularly the older people, who come here to get out of the house, to see people, have a good lunch. And then some of them will be forgetting their pin numbers and so on – and because we know them, we can help them out, tell them we'll settle it later or another day. And then you've got the allergies, and you get to know who's gluten free and so on and we know these people, so we work on it. I've now got my gluten free gravy to the point where it is a delicacy.'

We're sat on Table One in the corner of the Cabin this lunch-time, with people coming in and out as we speak. To underline the point, Paul comments 'that's the retired vicar who's just walked out', with a nod towards the door. 'And then the table of four over there were also church people – the archdeacon of Brecon, who's a real foodie, and friends. They come here often – a little while ago they had a meal here and then they were off to London to have dinner at Ottolenghi's!'

On a fine October evening I get a text from Paul and join him, Jean and some friends of theirs harvesting their potato fields, four acres of south-west sloping fields a mile or so from the sea on fine red sandstone soil. The sun is slowly setting over the estuary, light-ing up the dappled clouds above as I jump up to Paul's tractor.

'These are all Wilja. Boiling potatoes these are, but they can be chippers too. We had to use them last year because of the summer drought – they did end up making lovely chips though. Might be our soil – they do grow differently on different soil types. But then the rows we harvested the other day are Maris Piper, a classic chipping potato.'

They have already been out harvesting for a few hours when I join them; two tractors, one hauling a potato harvester and the other hauling a trailer gradually filling up with tonnes of potatoes to be stored and used over the next year at the Cabin. I scramble up to join Jean, Paul's dad, and two friends on top of the harvester, where they are picking out loose stones, rotten potatoes and clods from amongst the potatoes as they pass along the conveyor. You need quick eyes, and quick hands to pick out the unwanted bits from amongst the endless flow of potatoes rattling by. I join in for one row – 15 minutes or so – but even so my eyes are swimming with potatoes by the end. You learn one thing though; a potato's a potato and a stone's a stone.

Most years they harvest 40–50 tonnes of spuds from these fields. That keeps the Cabin going for a year, and gives them feed for cattle on top – as well as some to use as seed potatoes for the following year. 'We store the harvest in sheds for the winter. But then you get temperatures fluctuating in the winter – and we are definitely seeing more and more of that these days – and that affects the sugar and starch content, which affects their use in the kitchen and flavour on the plate. So if the chips are going dark, it means the temperature is too high, the sugar levels are high in the potato and it ends up sweeter.'

I ask him to tell me more about what it takes to make the perfect chip. 'Well, first there's the variety of potato. You do need to use a variety that is a good chipper, and it needs to be stored well. And then a lot of the skill in cooking is regulating the oil temperature. I'll not tell you the exact temperature we use but it's got to be in the range of 155–75C. The oil you use will affect the flavour of your food, as will the temperature you use it at and how frequently you change it. If you take your temperature too high you'll have to change your oil too frequently – and that's wasteful, particularly as you can't really process it for biodiesel any more. But on the other hand, I did talk to a chippy down the Gower a few years ago; I asked him how often he changed his oil and he was affronted, "I've been here for 26 years and I haven't changed my oil yet!" It was a tourist area, mind, so he got away with it.'

'But when you've got those things right you're looking at a centimetre square and ten centimetres long for your perfect chip. You fry it till it has some sort of rigidity – it shouldn't go limp on your plate – and till it's almost crispy, but also soft inside. Then you add your salt and vinegar and you're off. Golden perfection.'

As Paul says – and like many other fish and chip places across Wales – Ferry Cabin is not a fish and chip shop. And a perusal of their menu just as much as a chat with Paul confirms how true that is. Genuinely home-made crumbles, cakes and puddings sit in the dessert fridge. There are café classics – gammon, jacket potato, sandwiches. In pride of place at the top of the menu, alongside cawl and fish and chips, is a range of pies made with their own beef. They have 250 head of Hereford cattle on the farm, and all their pies and much else is made with their own beef; they had originally bought the place because there was no money in farming. But to create a market for your own produce by buying and running a café is a solution not many farmers would be able to pull off.

I ask Paul about their other suppliers. He rattles the answer off. 'Our milk comes from the farm dairy in Cwmffrwd, five miles up the road. Our eggs are all from local suppliers, vegetables are from north Carmarthenshire. Actually, we used to get our veg from a market gardener in the village, but then he retired. Our bacon and gammon are all from West Wales. We stick with the same suppliers, see – most of ours we've had for twenty years, because that way we know what we're getting, the customers know what they're getting and you've got the relationship. For fish we use DJ Foods for what we can't get locally – like cod or plaice – and then also some of the village fishermen for fish from the bay here and the estuary. Locally we used to be able to get sewin, salmon, sea bass, mullet, flatfish (or dabs as we call them), mackerel – and then bream and gurnard further out in the deeper water. But all that has gone down precipi- tously – we've not even had mackerel in the bay here for five years now. This is a famous salmon and sewin river – and they're almost all gone now. When I was growing up you could go down to the river in May and get 120 sewin in your net any day of the month. You wouldn't get that in a whole season now.'

Both saltwater and freshwater fishing have a long history in Wales, with the bounty of the seas and rivers providing abundantly throughout history up until the depredations of the twentieth century. The word 'abundant' here is entirely appropriate: within living memory there were shoals of herring in Cardigan Bay that were three miles long – today they don't get larger than 100 yards.[11] Go further back and the shoals, if anything, were even larger. In the 1740s, there were 97 small sloops registered along the coast between Aberdyfi and New Quay. During a single night in 1745, 1,386,500 herring were brought into the harbour in Aberystwyth.[12] Similar catches were recorded at other times from other fishing ports not just along the Welsh coast but in other parts too. The abundance was real enough; it's just that it was fragile.

Herrings, generally unpopular today, are assumed to be an indicator of poverty. In fact, the opposite seems to have been the case in Wales. The German geographer Herman Moll gave a description of the harbour at Aberystwyth in 1724, where he states that 'the herring fishery here is so exceedingly abundant that a thousand barrels have been taken in one night ... In addition to Herring they have such an abundance of cod, pollack, whiting, common whiting, ray and other fish that they set but little value on them.' In other words, the Welsh preference for herring and mackerel above other fish was the product not of scarcity but of a surfeit of choice.[13] Inland, a similar pattern can be seen in the historic predilection for sewin, salmon and trout, all widely regarded as the finest river fish and thus unsurprisingly considered the pick of the lot amongst the Welsh. These were almost always fried in butter or bacon fat; the very best way of course, to prepare oily fish of this sort.[14]

While Paul is reflecting on these worrying changes in the ecology of the river Tywi, and as if entirely pre-planned, an older man walks into the Cabin and Paul beckons him over. 'This is Brian,' he says, 'he's one of the old fishing boys.' I ask them both to tell me more about the fish, and what they'd put the decline down to. 'The seasons are changing massively,' says Paul, 'used to be, you could know exactly when the salmon would come up the river, same week every year. Now it varies and sometimes it's November before they come up.' But they also point out slurry run-off from farms getting into the water – 'some of those farmers don't mind because the fine they get for doing that sort of thing is cheaper than paying for the work of sorting it out, so they just keep doing it'. And then there's all the malformed fish, in much greater quantities than had ever previously been the case – 'like flat fish with four eyes', Brian grimaces. The consensus is that the contraceptive pill – and perhaps other chemicals and drugs in the water system – might well be responsible for this. 'And then you get a lot of illegal fishing – dredging – out in the bay. And the people responsible, those trawlers from Spain that come at night, get away with it.' One of these things by itself would be bad enough, but the combination of factors, here as elsewhere, is pushing entire ecosystems over the edge.

When Brian leaves, Paul explains to me that even putting all of that to one side, the old fishing tradition here is dying on its feet. 'When we started the Cabin, there were nine fishing licences in the village. Now there are three, and Brian is one of those. The old boys are retiring, no-one is taking their place – and then you've also got the fish disappearing, and the ones you do get are smaller. And that's partly because they're caught younger – too young.'

The abiding impression Paul leaves me with is that everything he does is intentional. In the way he farms, using the cattle manure to fertilize the potato fields, feeding the waste potatoes back to the cows and minimizing external inputs. In the way he has created a market for his produce by buying and running a café in his own village. In the way he cooks and stocks the café, going for quality and home produce but without going for an 'artisan' cachet that would alienate a lot of the locals. And in the way he would berate me for writing this paragraph, and insist, rightly, that all of this is him and Jean together.

As a result of all this, Ferry Cabin is in many ways a condensed microcosm of many of the food institutions that have played a central part in Welsh life for a hundred and fifty years, whilst also being very much its own thing. Village pubs, cafés and ice cream parlours established throughout the country by Italian immigrants, fish and chip shops – all independent businesses, rooted in their communities and all locally run. Husband and wife teams, mates in business together, long-established family concerns. All have made an essential contribution to the fabric of life in Wales. They are places where strong social webs are reinforced by an economic web where the pound circulates locally – to the part-time bar or café staff, the village plumber, the regional brewery. Places where chance encounters with familiar faces happen, and social bonds are strengthened in the small talk and joking banter.

Food lies at the very centre of this, and of all foods, chips are what links all those eateries. Chips are the potato made irresistible. Moreish bites that fill a hole by tantalizing taste buds. A takeaway wrapped in paper for £1.50 – dinner on the go – or served as a side to fish and salad in an upmarket establishment with sea views for £14. I have yet to meet anyone in Wales who genuinely dislikes chips.

Paul can have the last word. 'The simplicity of food has been lost. People put in too many flavours these days, and then you end up not being able to taste the fish – or the meat – or whatever it is, really.'

Cawl

Berwa dy gig y bore, – yna dod
Dy datws a'th lysie,
Toc o fara gydag e
A chaws, beth mwy 'chi eisie?

Dic Jones

There's only one house nearby
Hunkering down under Garn Fawr
Dolgaer its name, an old barn of a place
But a great spot for a welcome and a cuppa
Or even a bowlful of cawl. Now that's better food, with
Leeks and taters and stars on its face.
You can see the cauldron on its tripod
And the gorse crackling underneath.
They'll give you a ladle-full, and then another
The whole lot finer than any fancy mix;
You'll have a wooden spoon in the bowl as well
And a great big chunk of a ripe old cheese

From 'Pwllderi' by Dewi Emrys

9

CENNIN / LEEKS

May is upon us with its endless blue and the oaks and beeches are donning their mantles of vibrant green as we walk up the track to Blaencamel farm. It's my last visit for this book and my three-year-old daughter, holding my hand, is old enough for the first time to come with me to this most remarkable of Welsh farms. We spend the afternoon with Anne Evans and Peter Segger, who over the last 45 years have made this place with its poor soils into one of the most productive patches of earth in the whole of Wales, by growing organic vegetables on a commercial scale in a place where everyone said they couldn't. Of course, in reality there is nothing particularly novel in what they are doing; all farming was organic until a century ago, and it's not for nothing that the national emblem is a leek and that the national dish, *cawl*, is full of vegetables. But in continuing an ancient tradition and laying essential foundations for the future in doing so, Blaencamel seems to encapsulate so much of what I have been discovering about the value of food heritage for the future, and the need to defy the odds.

The leek is the Welsh vegetable par excellence, a garden staple that came to epitomize a country and its cuisine; this book could have easily been called *Laverbread, lamb and leeks* and we would have successfully ticked all the stereotype boxes. As usual, there is some justification to the stereotype. Leeks are not only an important ingredient in Welsh food historically but are also one of the national symbols of Wales. They are a core ingredient in cawl, imparting much of the flavour and the nutritional benefit, and there are centuries of culinary and cultivation history behind leeks and other vegetables in Wales. Many other iconic dishes – Glamorgan sausages, faggots and onions, *tato rhost* and a wide range of pies and stews – depend on a range of leafy and root vegetables, which despite their sometimes humdrum familiarity are both flavoursome and versatile and have been appreciated as such for centuries. But all this has become an untold story, as vegetable production in the country of the leek found itself completely relegated to the margins of farm life and food production.

The Welsh leek

Blaencamel grows leeks on a field scale and they try to have leeks available more or less year-round. Part of the reason for this is the ongoing demand for leeks, as there continues to be for all the other cawl vegetables – carrots, turnips, swede, onions, potatoes and parsnips. 'When we were starting up in the late 1970s, I remember the older people from round here coming to buy their cawl veg', Anne reminisces. 'That demand is as strong as ever, and I'd say the younger people are buying for cawl too, no doubt about that.'

We can't follow the interesting plot-twists in all the vegetables in cawl – colour-shifting carrots and 'newfangled' turnips, for example – but the story of Welsh leeks is a good central thread in this wider vegetable tale, not least for its symbolic connotations. The humble leek's status as the national symbol of Wales seems the most natural thing in the world to most British people, until you stop to think about it. Why, in fact, should a country be associated with a particular vegetable in the first place? Many countries have a national flower, and some even have a national fruit. But none bar Wales tout a vegetable as a defining symbol of nationhood. In some instances, the origin of the symbol is associated with some historic event, as in England's rose and the ascendancy of the house of Tudor, and in others because the plant or animal in question is particularly widespread in the country, as in Scotland's thistle, Dutch tulips and Swedish elks. The Welsh leek seems to have a little of both.

The leek's status as emblematic of Wales is no recent fancy; its use as a national symbol of sorts by the Welsh extends back to the post-Roman period. This era was foundational in the development of Welsh language and identity, and a significant proportion of the records that survive from this era are to do with the early saints – travelling Christian missionaries. Among these was one Saint David (*Dewi Sant*), whose feast-day of 1 March has become Wales's national day, and is also Wales's old leek-wearing day. This custom was already in evidence by the early 17th century, as an anonymous ballad explains for the perhaps bemused folk east of Offa's Dyke:

> For Englishmen Saint George,
> Saint Andrew for the Scot,
> Saint Patericke for Ireland,
> Saint David Welshmens Lot:
> In honour of which Saint,
> those Countrey men doe seeke,
> For to remember the same day,
> in wearing of a Leeke.[1]

By 1805, it had clearly become an unremarkable annual custom, familiar enough that leeks were worn even in church on St David's Day services, as a report from that year in the *Cambrian* newspaper confirms: '[the company] walked thence in procession, all in new clothing, and *wearing leeks*, to St Martin's Church. Prayers were read in the ancient British language, by the Rev. Thomas Alban ...'.[2] But the roots of this tradition of leek-wearing on 1 March seem to have less to do with St David himself than with later military encounters and the more prosaic fact that leeks have always been widely grown in Wales and are very much in season around St David's Day.

The earliest of these battles is one reputed to have happened between the forces of King Cadwallon (or perhaps his son, Cadwalader ap Cadwallon) of Gwynedd against invading Saxon forces somewhere on Welsh territory, and pertinently, near a field or patch of leeks, which could therefore be conveniently used as identifiers. A similar account is told of the Battle of Crécy in 1346, where Welsh soldiers fought alongside the Black Prince of England against France, with the idea again that the Welsh wore leeks as a distinguishing marker. The latter account, however, may have been embellished by the antiquarian Iolo Morganwg in the 18th century.[3] We are on firmer ground however by the time Shakespeare wrote his play *Henry V*, where in the first scene of Act V the archetypal Welsh character, Fluellen, exclaims: 'If your Majesty is remembered of it, the Welshmen did good service in a garden where leeks did grow, wearing leeks in their Monmouth caps, which your Majesty knows, to this hour is an honourable badge of the service, and I do believe, your Majesty takes no scorn to wear the leek upon Saint Tavy's day.' Here, the wearing-leeks-in-battle tradition and the St David's Day leek tradition are united, and the text is written in such a way as to imply that this Welsh practice of leek wearing is one Shakespeare's audience would be expected to know about. Clearly, therefore, by the 16th century at the latest, wearing leeks on Saint David's Day (or Saint Tavy's day, as rendered here) was a known Welsh tradition.

This is where biology and climate re-enter the tale, for the one unambiguous link between leeks and Saint David's Day that was as true in the Middle Ages as it is today is the fact that leeks are in season in Wales in early spring. As such, they are an important source of vitamin C during the so-called spring 'hungry gap'. In pre-modern European societies sourcing green vegetables during this time of year was a challenge, with new green growth generally scarce after the long winter dark, but the further west you travel in northern Europe, the milder the winters are, and the earlier spring arrives. This is a particularly important fact in understanding why leeks have long been considered so Welsh; away from the higher hills and mountains, winters in Wales tend to be wet, windy, and mild and dominated by moist air-masses from the Atlantic. Frost comes and goes, but prolonged cold spells and deep freezes are relatively uncommon, in sharp contrast to most parts of continental Europe. As gardeners know, this means that a good number of plants, including many root vegetables and leeks, can stand the winter outside in the garden in most western parts of the UK to an extent that is simply impossible further east in Europe. This fact has been remarked upon for centuries, often in connection with discussions of scurvy – a disease caused by lack of vitamin C in the diet from green vegetables. The Welsh aristocrat William Vaughan (1575–1641) had an estate in Carmarthenshire's Tywi Valley and a townhouse in London, and in a treatise on health published in 1630, commented that 'we in Wales have less frost and snow than those in London and Essex'.[4] In common with the prevailing view at the time, he thought this accounted for the comparative lack of scurvy he found among his neighbours in Carmarthenshire, but he had overlooked the missing link: the milder winters allowed them to incorporate greenstuff (green vegetables including leeks and cabbages) into their diet most of the year.

Without any understanding of the science behind scurvy, our ancestors seem to have learnt from experience the importance of greenstuff in the diet from prehistoric times and used a mixture of wild and cultivated plants in their diet and cooking to this end. The *allium* family, which includes leeks, onions, garlic and their wild relatives, are particularly useful to this end in Wales, Ireland and south-western parts of Britain. The wild members of this family grow abundantly in these Atlantic parts of the British Isles, and include wild garlic (*craf y geifr*) which grows prolifically, carpeting woodland floors with delicious, tangy green leaves for the pot from late February through to May. Their relative, the wild leek, is also native to more sheltered parts of Wales and the culturally related Cornish coast, and produces very useful winter leaves here, while it is notably absent from areas in central or eastern England or indeed in any areas further east on the continent where winters are colder.

Unlike wild garlic, however, this 'wild' leek itself seems to have been given a helping hand in its colonization efforts by humans. This now naturalized plant is regarded as having been introduced to Britain from areas further south in Europe by early human settlers, in all likelihood at some point long before written records begin.[5] There is strong evidence for this in Wales and it suggests that the use of leeks in Welsh cooking predates even the earliest written records. Although comparatively rare today, it is striking that those sites where the wild leek is found are usually also sites of ruined settlements and ancient field systems – at South Stack in Anglesey, for instance, it is found growing near a group of prehistoric hut circles.[6] It's impossible to know for sure but it seems likely from this that the ancient Welsh were using both wild leeks and wild garlic in their cooking long before the Romans introduced the related cultivated variety, which originates in the eastern Mediterranean.

At any rate, by the time the native Welsh laws were written in the 9th century there was enough vegetable cultivation for the laws to include regulations for farmers to fence their fields and gardens, and leeks – along with cabbages – are one of the few crops singled out for mention by name.[7] Linguistic evidence in Middle Welsh supports this picture of fairly widespread vegetable cultivation, with the now archaic word 'lluarth' – meaning vegetable garden – appearing frequently in medieval texts, along with 'gardd fresych' for cabbage garden. Leek cultivation during this period left its legacy, unsurprisingly, in Welsh place names, with the village of Cilcennin, 'Leek patch', a stone's throw up the valley from Blaencamel farm, and Llanbedr-y-Cennin in the north-east; both locations too far inland for wild leeks to grow.

Of course, none of this yet accounts for why leeks became so strongly associated with Wales; Anglo-Saxon England also had its *leac-garth* (leek gardens) and leeks were widely grown in medieval Europe.[8] The change seems to have come with the growth in horticulture from the 16th century onwards. By the 1620s, as the fashionable classes of England started to enjoy exciting new foods such as cucumbers and spinach – often introduced via the Netherlands – leeks started to fall out of favour. The need for leeks as a winter vegetable was also reduced by the introduction of pickled vegetables (always more popular from this point on in more challenging areas for winter vegetable cultivation such as eastern England or Germany, compared to milder areas such as Wales or France) and by the middle of the 17th century, leeks remained in use only among the poorest people in England. In Wales, however, leeks continued to be ubiquitous, and even the gentry stuck with the old favourite.[9] The same shift seems to have taken place on the continent, relegating leeks to the status of second-class vegetable, beloved only of the Swiss.[10] Two centuries later, a report writer could still note that there was 'scarcely a cottage garden in Siluria (Glamorganshire, Monmouthshire, &c.) without a proportionate large bed of leeks; some of which are earthed up like celery; and thereby are blanched, and rendered mild and tender: to be used not only as a condiment, but sometimes as an aliment'.[11] This use of leeks as an 'aliment', or a core foodstuff, is undoubtedly an allusion to their use in these cottages, alongside other vegetables, in cawl.

Cawl

The etymological root of the word 'cawl' lies in the Latin for 'stick or stem of a plant, cabbage-stick, cabbage', and from there the word came to be used for a stew in which greenstuff was present. By the 15th century, the Welsh word 'cawl' was used by the physicians of Myddfai to denote a liquid that could be drunk, often translated into English as 'pottage'. Even if the origins of cawl lie with cabbages, leeks have long been one of its principal ingredients, essential for imparting flavour. David Thomas's 18th century ditty on the customs of the thirteen counties of Wales explicitly links 'cawl cennin', 'leek broth' with Glamorgan and Monmouthshire. Other vegetables used in modern 'lamb cawl' were also widely used; Carmarthenshire and Cardiganshire are associated with 'cawl erfin', turnip or swede soup, in the same poem. We get a detailed description of what went into a normal family's cawl by the early 19th century from the English traveller, Heath Malkin. On his fashionable tour of romantic Wales in 1804, he describes the diet of rural cottages in Glamorgan:

Broths made from all sorts of meat are much used; in which large quantities of potherbs and other vegetables form a principal ingredient; abundance of leeks, onions, shalots, parsley, savoury, pennyroyal, marjoram, thyme, cresses, beets, lettuces, spinach, and other productions of the garden. Herb broth, as it is called, is much used by the common people ... and [they] take it with bread.

From all these accounts we have further evidence that leeks continued to be widely cultivated in Wales – or at the very least in south-eastern counties – even in the centuries after they had fallen out of fashion elsewhere, and the fondness for cawl as a dish seems to have had a part to play in that. It is also clear that, like many other peasant dishes, cawl historically wasn't one dish with a set ingredients list, but more a type of dish with a range of possible options. These differing versions of cawl were the mainstay of most people's diets throughout the country until the 20th century, and always made heavy use of vegetables. Perhaps because of this, the writer Meg Dodds noted in 1826 that 'the French take the lead of all European people in soups and broths, the Scotch rank second, the Welsh next, and the English are at the very bottom of the scale'.

Most people would agree, however, that somewhere near the middle of that range of possibilities lies this classic recipe from Ceredigion. The recipe calls for a joint each of bacon and either mutton or beef, along with swede, carrots, cabbage, potatoes, leeks, parsley, oatmeal and water. The joints of meat are put together into a large saucepan and boiled for at least an hour. The root veg are then added and boiled for 15 minutes or so before the potatoes are put in. This is then allowed to boil further so that the juices and flavours start merging, and the leek and a small amount of parsley are added ten minutes or so before serving. In a similar twist to traditional variants of the Marseillaise bouillabaisse (fish stew), where the fish and the broth are served separately, the broth in a cawl of this sort is usually served clear, with the vegetables and meat dished up as a second course. The best cawl, like well-matured wine or cheese, is best served reheated and eaten the day after it is first made, so that all the flavours have time to seep into each other and become a culinary masterpiece of peasant cookery, rightly praised.

Glamorgan Sausages

But cawl was not the only destination for vegetables, and it is striking that, at least during this period before the industrial revolution had taken off in earnest, vegetables were much in evidence even in poorer people's diets. A series of reports into agriculture in Wales published in the 1810s by the poet Walter Davies (Gwallter Mechain) paints a good picture of what was grown in the burgeoning market garden enterprises in his reports into agriculture in South Wales. According to one report, the most important centre of market gardening in the Cardiff area, for instance, had become Llandaff:

> The kitchen-gardens of the market-men at Llandaff, near Cardiff, are numerous and productive; supplying the most convenient parts of South Wales, and in a certain proportion the Bristol market, with vegetables: such a group of gardens for the accommodation of the public, we have not noticed elsewhere within the district. To enumerate the several articles of the first-rate gardens, would be to write in part a botanical dictionary: the crops of a farmer's garden consist of the vegetables most appropriate to his table, viz. early potatoes, yellow turnips, early and winter cabbages, greens, varieties of peas and beans, carrots, onions, and other alliaceous plants, and varieties of salads; to which some add broccoli, cauliflowers, asparagus, seakale, rhubarb.

The range of vegetables listed here is by Davies's own admission only a part of what was known and grown. The presence of asparagus, broccoli and salads on his list may go some way to dispelling some tired notions of historic Welsh fare, and tells us that a good range of vegetables were grown by this period for uses other than cawl. Some of these uses included *tatws pum munud* and *tatws popty* (described on pages 124 and 181), faggots, pies and Glamorgan sausages.

The last of these have earned not a little fame in recent decades as an apparently traditional 'vegetarian sausage', made using leeks and cheese. Exactly how long this has been the case is open to dispute. The first known reference to a Glamorgan sausage seems to have been in a personal notebook kept by a certain John Perkins around the year 1800, where the sausages certainly contain pork. By the 1850s the travel writer George Borrow on his journey through Wales could quip that 'Glamorgan sausages, [are] I really think are not a whit inferior to those of Epping' – Epping sausages being skinless, meat-based sausages. Like many regional English sausages, these sausages seem to have contained meat, but also a range of local flavourings. Although the notes in Perkins's notebook don't include a reference to leeks, they do call for cloves and sage.

By the 1870s regular adverts were appearing in local newspapers for Glamorgan sausages, some of which state that they are made from 'choice dairy-fed pork'; again no mention of leeks, but an unusual link with dairy produce.[12] Although, in 1905, the Weekly Mail could confidently publish that 'one hears nothing now about Glamorgan sausages. Fifty years ago they were a speciality of the county', the tradition must have continued in some form as the sausages seem to have seen a resurgence in popularity during the rationing of the Second World War. In the 1950s the Welsh Gas Board was able to publish a cookbook in which the sausage was entirely vegetarian and the recipe included both cheese and leeks – all this without causing local outcry. Even in the absence of a stable and unchanging recipe, it is very possible that the sausage's lineage contained both leek and cheese, as both ingredients are known to have been commonly available in Glamorgan historically. Regardless, it was in this form that the Glamorgan sausage became in the latter half of the 20th century a regular feature on pub and food festival menus throughout Wales, bringing a hint of heritage to the vegetarian food scene. As with so much else in food, the historic basis for this traditional vegetarian staple is shaky; but the myth is powerful and encapsulates many foods' shifting identities.

But though Welsh cottage gardens provided ample leeks for Glamorgan sausages, cawl and so many other dishes, onions were another matter. They could be grown in gardens, but the desire among Welsh housewives who worked with them to have the very best quality onions (which are of course related to leeks) led to the development of an iconic and surprising cross-channel and cross-cultural cottage industry.

Sioni Winwns

It's a fine early autumn day in Llantwit as I cycle the final approach into town in September 2010. People are milling around the string of small shops and a couple of older women are stood chatting to a man whose bike is leaning against a lamppost. I lock my bike and amble over; he is indeed wearing a striped shirt and his bike is laden with strings of onions. I'm delighted, and greet him in French. He's a student from Brittany; yes, he's been here a few weeks – there's a small team of them with a base in Cardiff selling in the towns round about. This is one of the modern Sioni Winwns (known in English as Onion Johnnies), selling Breton onions in Wales in an unbroken tradition extending back to the 1820s.

I buy a string from him, and hand them to Mam when I get back that afternoon. She's delighted; she hadn't seen any Sionis in Cardiff yet that year, but the onions are so much better than the ones you get in the shops – sweeter, and they keep better. She remembers a previous generation of Sionis as a fixture of the Pontypridd streetscape in the 1970s. That generation was not composed of students, partly spending their time in Wales in order to improve their English. In fact, there were generations of Sionis selling in Wales who not only didn't speak English but were hardly able to get by in French either: these were bilingual Breton-Welsh market farmers, whose market just happened to be located several hundred miles of sea travel away from their homes.

Sioni Winwns / Ar Joniged / Onion Johnnies: the name originally refers to a group of small, peasant farmers from a handful of villages in the Rosko area of northern Brittany who sold their local onions in Britain, starting in 1828. The soil and climate of their part of Brittany are well-suited to vegetable growing, and the local farmers had the advantage of a notably sweet, pink variety of onion, originally brought over by monks from Portugal. In the context of Breton poverty in post-Napoleonic France, with a rapidly industrializing UK (and Wales at the very forefront of this), there was a clear economic incentive to test the market overseas, even if this meant months away from home for the farmers. The timing worked in terms of the onion season – each year sown in February, harvested in July, leaving August – January as the selling season in Britain.

The gamble paid off, and as the UK further loosened import restrictions on food through the 1840s, the door was opened to the Sionis to make the most of this burgeoning market. By 1860 there were 200 Sionis making the journey over to sell in Britain; by 1887 this number had grown to 700 and at the high watermark in 1931, there were 1,500. And although these Johnnies found their way to towns and cities everywhere from Plymouth to Shetland, there was always a disproportionately large number of them in Wales; and the tradition of selling in Wales continued longer than anywhere else, with the Cardiff team continuing as other areas fell by the wayside.

For the Sionis, Wales was a natural destination. Partly this is to do with language, and partly with the market they found there (though the two things are not unrelated). Broad swathes of both Brittany and Wales were monolingual Breton- and Welsh-speaking until the Second World War, and the two languages are closely related, though not quite to the point of mutual intelligibility. The myth of Sionis selling their onions in Breton to housewives who replied in Welsh doesn't quite hold true, but the similarity between the languages allowed the Bretons to pick up functional Welsh within weeks, and complete fluency often within a season or two of visiting. As sellers usually returned to the same area year after year, they picked up the Welsh dialect of their patch, be that Llanelli, Newcastle Emlyn, Porthmadog or even London, thanks to the Ceredigion dairymen and women who had settled there.

And the market they found in Wales was a ready one, thanks to Welsh housewives' good nose for an onion. As we've seen, Wales had experienced early and rapid industrialization, with significant population growth through the 19th century, and it also had peasant cooking traditions that made great use of the onion family of vegetables, whose main guardians and cooks were housewives. The thing about onions is that they aren't an essential part of anyone's diet, but they add depth of flavour to almost any cooked dish, and particularly soups and stews. Urban and rural poverty didn't affect the fact that onions were readily available at the market everywhere in Wales, and were commonly grown in back gardens with leeks. But the Rosko pink onion, with its fine flavour and good keeping qualities was markedly superior to the onions grown in miners' gardens and farmers' veg patches in Wales, and to those available at market stalls. The ready market that Sionis found in Welsh mining towns and rural farm holdings alike testify to the miners' and farmers' wives good taste, and their recognition of a quality vegetable, worth spending money on, when they saw one. So this story, as much as it is about Breton cuisine, is a tale of Welsh food culture. As the sellers returned year by year to their patch, cycling even to remote farmhouses on their onion-laden bikes, they became an established part of the food landscape, and their arrival was expected and anticipated.

Until the last of the traditional, seasonal sellers retired in the 1990s, many of the Sionis' main income source lay in selling onions in Britain. They spent decades travelling back and forth seasonally between Brittany and Great Britain, with a familiar 'home' in their seasonal selling base (usually an old warehouse or shop where they slept with their onions) and a home and family in Brittany. If Brexit puts paid to the Sioni trade in Wales – and the last Sionis in Tregaron in autumn 2019 said they wouldn't be returning after Brexit – it will have sadly managed to kill off a tradition that survived two world wars and lasted over a hundred and eighty years, linking two countries and food cultures with an allium.[13] My own Mam was surely echoing what generations of Welsh mothers had told their children on many an autumn Saturday when she'd tell me, *gwna'n siwr bod ti'n cael winwns gan Sioni os weli di un!* ('Make sure you get onions from Sioni if you see one').

Blaencamel

'Can you provide a year-round vegetarian diet for Wales today with veg grown in Wales?' A simple, but perhaps revolutionary question. Anne paused; 'When we started here in the early 70s everyone said – including the locals, mind you – that it was impossible. Not just feeding the nation with organically grown local vegetables, but even making a living on a farm in this area by growing vegetables.' Anne's words take me to the heart of Wales's vegetable paradox: the country of the leek, with a strong culinary tradition of vegetable use and many early ventures in market gardening, was by the end of the 20th century only producing the tiniest fraction of the fresh fruit and veg consumed in the country. I know full well that this state of affairs has come about in no small part due to the dictates of an economic orthodoxy that has contributed enormously to the developing climate crisis, and that has also left Wales's many small farmers, like those of so many other parts of the world, in semi-perpetual crisis. So I am keen to learn how Blaencamel, this 50-acre farm in Ceredigion's Aeron valley, has managed to become a fifty-year-old Welsh veg success story against all the odds. And I have a personal interest in walking these fields, as most of the veg I ate as a teenager in Cardiff would have been grown there, thanks to my mother's decision to sign up in the early days of the farm's veg box scheme.

The first thing that strikes me as I walk up the track with my daughter in the brilliant May sunshine are the greenhouses; one-and-a-half acres of them, to be precise. These provide the key marginal gains in terms of temperature and weather protection that allow Blaencamel to produce many vegetables pretty much 52 weeks a year. Among those are a full range of salads, kale, spinach, chard, beetroot and, with a 6-week gap, carrots. When we catch up with Peter, I remark that this is a far cry from most people's ideas of the potential of vegetable growing in Wales. 'Yes, when we started people said they'd give us three or four years and we'd be gone. It is true that our vision always veered towards the idealistic,' Peter muses as we survey a field with half an acre of young leeks, 'in that we were trying to grow veg on almost impossible land at a time when "organic" was practically unknown so didn't get a premium, and we had a business model dependent on selling this produce to local shops. But one way or another, we got through.'

In the early years, they had the advantage of a rural customer base who were very familiar with eating and cooking seasonally, and who were used to the crops that do well in the climate. The leeks have just been planted out on the day we visit, and leeks were in fact a money-maker for the farm in the early days, quite apart from the strong demand for them as cawl ingredients. The trick was to find out when Welsh rugby internationals were held in Cardiff. Rugby being a winter sport, match days like the Six Nations in January – March, tended to be held when leeks were in season. 'It was great for us,' Peter chuckles, 'we'd load the van full of leeks and tank down to Cardiff. Now when people are looking for a leek as a symbol of their nationality, you're charging per leek rather than by the pound or the bunch. So a pound a leek or two pounds for a leek doesn't make too much of a difference for the rugby fan who's already had a pint or two. Best of all if it's a monster leek, of course.'

We return to the topic of traditional vegetable crops in the area, and Peter brings up broad beans. 'The plants love it here! They've been grown in this area for centuries in people's back gardens, and when we started selling them the older people used to lap them up to boil at home and then serve with butter on bread.' This is of course in one sense very simple, peasant food – but also tasty and a great vegetarian protein source. They have seen some of those ways of eating change though, and in no small part put it down to supermarkets. Peter explains that because broad beans are so bulky they take space on display shelves and in lorries, and for the supermarkets' distribution systems that makes them expensive. So the chains decide they'd rather shift demand away from broad beans and start a ratchet effect where they put prices up and make the packs slightly smaller. As a result fewer people buy them, and so prices can go up further. 'Now broad beans are rare on supermarket shelves, but they ought to be abundant. We've been cheaper than the supermarkets for years for broad beans, but as a result of the chains' influence on people's buying and eating habits, the demand is nowhere near what it could be these days.'

Peter can speak with authority on supermarkets' internal logic, as he spent twenty years running a local co-operative that sold Blaencamel produce – amongst others – to supermarkets across the UK. The aim was to normalize organic food, and supermarkets seemed the best way to do it. This led Peter to twenty years of travel, across the UK and the world, trying to find organic producers who could supply everything that supermarkets might want to sell organically. It was a great chance to learn how they thought and what their requirements were for everything. 'The funny thing was how demand in those days still varied quite a bit by what part of the UK you were in. So in south-east England, people would only buy the white of the leek. Everything else was considered more or less waste. But in the Welsh valleys people wanted plenty of the green stuff, for cawl and for flavour. They were right of course. The green ends are also more nutritious, and they're probably part of the reason why leeks were just so popular historically here – you can grow them easily, harvest them through winter and spring and there is practically no waste. You eat the whole plant!'

But then soon after the turn of the millennium, they decided they needed to return to the original vision. 'If you're going to have a sustainable food economy – really sustainable for the long-term – you need to produce as much as you can locally. So we asked that question about what was really important to us to spend the rest of our lives doing, and the answer was soil, biodiversity, climate, energy, the economy; or in a word, good food.' They refocused their work on Wales, and on the original vision of selling to local people direct from the farm and supplying local food outlets. They wanted to look particularly at food imports and the environmental footprint of those imports, and see what could be done to replace them with vegetables grown in Wales.

Anne's obvious passion for this and the potential that lies in Welsh-grown agretti, squash or tomatoes reminds me of the market-gardeners of 1810 with their asparagus and broccoli. Both of them visionary enterprises exploring and introducing new foods to people's plates and palates, and both in different ways doing so in the teeth of the economic orthodoxy of their day. In the early nineteenth century vegetable growing in Britain wasn't considered serious agri-culture, and it was generally ignored in favour of cereal growing and livestock rearing.[14] Today, the potential of feeding Western societies through the kinds of low-input, intensive organic vegetable grow-ing that Blaencamel exemplifies is also ignored. It's an idea that lies well outside the economic mainstream, but Blaencamel proves it is more than possible. And as the English farmer and researcher Chris Smaje, amongst others, has demonstrated, a small farm future of this kind with vegetable growing at its centre could allow Britain to feed itself while both reducing carbon emissions and keeping alive the tradition of small family farms.[15]

The farm system used at Blaencamel is proof of this. Using

compost generated entirely from waste produced on the farm itself and some manure from neighbouring livestock, a seven-year rotation and no outside input other than labour and seed, the farm produces enough vegetables to provide the entire neighbourhood with all their vegetable needs year-round. And it does all this on soil that is far from propitious for vegetable growing. Some parts of Wales are a veg-grower's dream, but the Aeron valley is not among them, as Peter demonstrates by picking up a handful of the silty soil from an unimproved field corner and rubbing it – it's a pale, slightly bleached colour and crumbly rather than friable in the way good, humus-rich soil would be. But the best fertilizer is the farmer's shadow, as the old saying has it, and the contrast between the poor base soil and the ploughed fields or the soil in the greenhouses, which have had decades of improvement through nothing more than compost and cultivation, is obvious even to an untrained eye.

So to argue that Wales is unsuited to vegetable cultivation on a farm scale is to assume that the current economic system, and its associated orthodoxy, is somehow normative for all that could or should happen in Welsh farming and to ignore the evidence of these outliers. Blaencamel grows 15 acres of field vegetables and gives seven local people long-term employment[16] – a much better job/acre ratio than for most farms. It also generates its income entirely from vegetable sales; there has been no diversification into holiday cottages, an onsite coffee shop or anything else. It's almost as if the Seggers want to make the point that, if it's viable here, how much more so could it be in areas with better soils, or with other potential income streams?

The other side of this virtuous coin that blows me away as we wander between the greenhouses and fields is seeing strawberries, courgettes and early potatoes in May, all produced without fossil fuels. In fact, the way they farm here is not only carbon-neutral, but carbon-negative, with carbon slowly locked into the farm soils year-on-year. This goes hand in hand with the biodiversity on the farm, spared the destruction of pesticide and fungicide pollution from the organic cultivation, and now providing substantial benefits to the farm's crops. This comes to light when I ask about the leek moth, an import from Asia which has made leek growing in gardens and allotments a nightmare, and put me off growing leeks in my own garden for years. 'We haven't had them yet, thank God', Peter answers. 'I don't know exactly why, but I have a few ideas. One thing is that we have this long rotation – we don't grow leeks in the same field for a full six years, and that helps prevent the build-up of diseases and pests in the soil by disrupting their life-cycles. But surely just as significant is the distance between the fields here, and the old high hedges and woodlands we have here, which make up 7–10 acres of the farm, depending on how you measure.' So as well as providing a haven for wildlife of all kinds, these semi-wild areas of the farm also form natural barriers, which have allowed the farm to continue growing leeks without yet suffering from this new climate-induced pest.

The leek's Welshness originally came about to a great extent because of its suitability for cultivation here. My daughter is familiar with full-grown leeks as a cawl ingredient from helping us in the kitchen, but when I point at the baby leeks growing in the field in Blaencamel shortly before we leave and ask her what it is, she doesn't know. That's because leeks aren't among the vegetables she is familiar with from our own garden, knocked off the list a few years ago because of the faff of growing them with leek moth around. As the climate changes, and leek moth is accompanied by allium leaf miners and other as yet unknown future pests, leeks may become unviable to grow in any quantity in Wales, and I wonder about the cawl that my daughter might prepare for her children or grandchildren in the 2050s or 2080s. Cawl started of course with cabbage, which slowly yielded its place to leeks. On my optimistic days, Anne's vision has come to fruition and Wales and other parts of the northern hemisphere have many more Blaencamels, growing the widest possible range of vegetables and locking in carbon as they do so. The long cawl tradition continues to evolve, incorporating new vegetables from other parts of the world, even as it retains a link to the past. As the decades go on and Wales, I earnestly hope, welcomes those who have lost their own homes and lands to the ravages of climate change, food will be an essential bridge between cultures. Just as Sioni Winwns came and enriched Welsh culture with their annual flogging of a pink onion, even as they learnt Welsh in order to do so, I hope that perhaps more permanent arrivals from other cultures in future will bring culinary contributions that continue the long story of Welsh foods, and not least vegetables.

The sun is slowly setting away to the west as we drive home, my daughter falling asleep as we zig-zag along the country lanes and I fully realize, perhaps for the first time, just how existential all this will be for her. If the Wales she grows up in is a place where the likes of Blaencamel, Felin Ganol, Tŷ Tanglwyst and the economic logic they represent become increasingly commonplace, it will be a vastly healthier, happier and richer place for her and all her generation. And by virtue of measuring riches in the currency of swallows in the sky and humane, rooted work available for so many more, it will surely also be a place doing vastly less damage to all its global neighbours, both alive and unborn. I leave pondering this with Anne's words ringing in my ears. 'All this is about health and the joy of food. Good food is critical for the culture of any society.'

POSTSCRIPT

My aim for this book was always to allow the long stories of some of the foods of Wales and the tales of the people producing them today to speak for themselves. I hope that in doing so, many of the threads I pointed out in the introduction – the effects of industrialization and the market economy on food, the importance of women, the wiles of fashion, the similarities and differences from neighbouring food cultures – have come to the fore sufficiently for the careful reader to ponder the implications for Wales's present and future, and also the food and farming futures of other Western societies. But in case I haven't succeeded in this, I'd like to expand on three reflections on the Welsh food story as a whole here.

My first is simply that, after four years' personal exploration of Welsh food, there is such a thing as a constellation of native foods in Wales that have both tradition and story behind them and that in their use together form a distinct culinary tradition – even a cuisine. This is not a mere statement of the obvious; an entirely separate book could be written no doubt on the history of the disparagement of the idea of 'Welsh food'. But cheese, shellfish, breads, cider, sheep's meat and much else have long been associated with Wales by both outsiders and natives, and have formed a major part of the eating habits of the Welsh. They are foods that can be produced without undue effort from this land, and together form all that is needed for a healthy and varied diet.

Part of this is the fact that this culinary tradition is also very much of this corner of Europe. By that I mean that, as would be true of any cuisine or food culture, none of the foodstuffs mentioned in this book are uniquely Welsh but belong to a particular strand of the world's culinary heritage that we can call European. Leavened bread is, famously, found in great variety across the continent, from the rye breads of Poland to the *papos secos* of Portugal. Cheese of all sorts is a speciality of European countries from Spain to Switzerland and the Netherlands. Salty butter is just as much part of the Breton food story as the Welsh one.

How can we understand this? It is true, for instance, that the ingredient list and smorgasbord of common dishes in this food tradition have much in common in particular with the fare of other mountainous regions of Europe but, then, we find a bounty of seafood that brings an entirely different twist to the menu. To have a penchant for cooked cheese, pairs Welsh fare with the peasant traditions of the Alps, as does a tradition of air-dried ham. Lamb is also a feature of mountainous diets (as are goat and mutton), uniting Wales with Norway and the Pyrenees. But oysters and cockles take us to the French and Iberian Atlantic coasts. Laver has a tradition behind it on the coasts of Scotland and Ireland. Cider on the other hand requires sheltered lowland with ample but not excessive rainfall, so uniting eastern Wales with parts of England, Normandy and western regions of Germany. And then a range of traditional grains, but with an emphasis on oats, brings us back to the windward Celtic landscapes of the British Isles.

Further reflection confirms the unsurprising observation that the family resemblance is closest to the cuisines of two countries in particular. These are neighbouring England and Ireland, the latter lying just within sight over the westward sea and sharing a related language and thousands of years of trade and petty warfare, the former just over Offa's Dyke and bound to Wales by centuries of political union and economic ties. But strikingly, even in comparison with both these near neighbours, we find notable divergences in food and farming practices and in what we can only call culinary preference. Compared with Ireland, the continental influences – which brought the cider tradition, for instance – had a much more marked effect on Welsh eating habits. Wales was also always richer than her western neighbour, partly as a result of the early cessation of warfare due to the early and brutal conquest by England and the wealthy markets that eventually opened up to the Welsh in England's large cities, and partly as a consequence of the industrialization that meant Wales's population actually grew during a period when both Ireland and Scotland were losing the bulk of their population through emigration. This general economic stability led to greater variety in many people's diet and to the adoption of new foods, particularly among wealthier lowland farmers and the aristocracy. So we find references to imports of figs, prunes and raisins into Welsh ports as early as the later Middle Ages, and by the 16th century recipe books and letters imply that imported spices, for instance, were just as familiar in well-off Welsh kitchens as they were in provincial England.[1]

In comparison with England, however, we still find stark differences in the baseline diet, reflecting different customs and preferences, many of which have much in common with historic Irish fare – the predominance of oats, the love of dairy and the general lack of beef all notable in this regard. Indeed, many of the best records we have of Welsh food historically came about through the phenomenon of English tourists visiting Wales in the search of the exotic and the romantic on their very doorstep, and commenting on the strange customs they found in the country. Yet despite all these numerous interesting and informative commonalities, Welsh food taken as a whole differs in noteworthy ways, as we have seen, from the cuisines of both nearest neighbours.

What can we say, then, other than that we have on our hands a western European cuisine, very much of the British Isles, that draws on a common range of ingredients and preparation methods, but does so in its own unique way? It is clear that the particular combination of foodstuffs and emphases in traditional Welsh food is one that simply doesn't occur elsewhere. Personally, I find it delicious.

This distinct culinary tradition deserves, in my humble but considered opinion, the moniker of a 'cuisine'. The core palette of ingredients is surprisingly broad for such a small area, not much larger in surface than the Belgian Walloon region. It is a mostly peasant tradition that has made use of the produce of the seas and rivers, shallow tidal waters, fertile valley soils and rocky hills that form this country. We find animal products, grains, vegetables and top fruit all making substantial contributions to the list. In other words, there is enough breadth here to allow for further development and new departures.

Secondly, and related to this, I hope that I have managed to persuade you that those same Welsh foods and dishes, in the enterprising hands of cooks, chefs, makers, bakers, farmers and brewers (today) and perhaps most of all housewives (yesterday) are worth exploring and getting to know. Quality is always worth seeking out. And that quality – despite everything and often little-trumpeted

– exists today in Wales, and most particularly in those foods that have been made and prepared from the land of Wales for long enough to be widely considered 'of this land'. The traditions that led to Caerphilly cheese or Welsh rarebit, to laverbread and Welsh cakes were organic developments over countless generations of the raw material that was available, and often abundant, on this large, hilly peninsula on an island in the north-west of Europe. In the right hands, these are true treats, reflected in the numerous accolades awarded those Welsh foodstuffs and dishes that are made to the highest standards by skilled producers.

But I realize this will not persuade all. A common charge levelled at the foods that feature both in Welsh cuisine and the cuisines of many neighbouring cultures are that they are heavy, even stodgy. There is some truth to this accusation: porridge, cawl, fish and chips and many of the other dishes mentioned in this book are filling meals better suited to people doing heavy physical work on a farm or in a mine than in front of a laptop screen. But this is in fact equally true of the vast majority of the traditional dishes of France, Italy or Spain, which are not often accused of being overly heavy: pasta, cassoulet and *caldo gallego* are not exactly light meals. Having spent several years following the contours of Welsh food history, it seems to me that the reason Welsh dishes and ingredients are not particularly present in restaurant fare or cookbooks today has more to do with their story not being told, than the innate unsuitability of the foods themselves for modern palates. *Cocos a wya* (see page 80), *llymru* (page 146) or Carmarthen ham (page 123) on a slice of sourdough bread with Welsh butter are just three examples from this book of entirely traditional Welsh dishes that would lend themselves perfectly to a modern light starter menu. Many other ingredients and traditional dishes that use heavy joints of meat or large quantities of grains or dairy can be paired with locally-grown salads to create lighter meals.

Above and beyond all this, there is a strong argument to use the best quality ingredients, paying a fair price for doing so, and to simply enjoy the sumptuousness of rich butter, laverbread or chips. As an old Welsh poet sang *Iôn a roes yn ein hoes ni / gynnyrch byd i'n digoni* ('The Lord has given us in our day / the world's food to enjoy'). Even as an occasional treat, surely the enjoyment derived from the salt/ fat/ sweet/ grain goodness of *Slapan* (page 149) or *Cig moch, caws a winwns* (page 124) is worth the splurge, if only to remind one's palate that such foods exist. And then the experience must be capped by washing everything down with an excellent single-variety Monmouthshire cider or even some *diodgriafol*, if somebody were to start producing it again.

The third thing that I hope has been implicitly obvious throughout the book is many of these food traditions have their own peculiar terminology and language, and that native language is Welsh. There is a specific vocabulary in Welsh – much neglected, and at risk of disappearance even among daily speakers of the language – to do with all the domains of food preparation from the specific minutiae of farming, to production, kitchen preparation and onto the table. Words like *pingo* (the verb used when a fruit tree is heavy-laden with fruit such that the branches are bending; it is said to be 'pingo'), *crafell* (an oatcake slice) or *mwtrin* (a mash including potatoes, swede and also carrot or peas, served usually with buttermilk) have disappeared from the vocabulary of most speakers under the age of 70. It goes almost without saying that even the concepts they embody have therefore also almost disappeared not only from Welsh-speaking culture but even more so from Anglo-Welsh culture. What has replaced many of these terms are simple calques[2] from the English, wiping away the rich language of dairy produce, with umpteen original terms for milk of different sorts, for instance, replaced with Anglicisms. So *llaeth crych* was milk about to turn to butter; *armel* the second milk, best for buttermaking, and *tical* the very last milk, considered even richer than the *armel*. None of these terms are now in common currency. Neither are words like *isgell* (stock), *llaeth glas* (skimmed milk) or *eirin Mair* (gooseberries), replaced by *stoc*, *llaeth sgim* and *gwsberis*. This is more than linguistic purism; this is what happens when an entire food culture is subsumed by the industrial food machine of the modern Western world.

This could, however, be changed: what has been almost lost can be un-lost. One important source of new richness for the modern Welsh food scene is the different perspectives and flavours brought for centuries by the presence of immigrant and ethnic minority communities. It is a little-known fact that one of the first purpose-built mosques built in the UK was in Cardiff in the early 20th century, thanks to the city's port.[3] There are records of sailors from Cape Verde in the city as early as the 17th century, and they were followed by Yemeni dockworkers who brought their families and flavours of home with them to the city before the 19th century was out. Italian migrants settled widely during the early 20th century across the cities and towns of industrial south Wales, establishing ice cream parlours and cafés that became local institutions and introducing new dishes and beverages, not least *cappuccino* under the guise of 'milky coffee'. These waves of immigration left their mark not only in the introduction of entirely new foods and ways of eating, as everywhere in the Western world, but also in novel combinations such as the Cardiff takeaway 'arf'n'arf' of chips and rice. Other outside influences brought the familiar sight of Breton onion sellers to Wales every summer, as we have seen. More recently, English back-to-the-land migrants have re-established viable veg-growing enterprises in areas where they had disappeared and have been instrumental in establishing the burgeoning Welsh wine industry. The threads these communities and influences have brought to the story of Welsh food in and of themselves deserve further explanation, and it is enticing to think of the possibilities that could arise from a marriage between them and a revival of the older, native traditions.

In sum, then, we have here: firstly, a group of native foods and dishes; secondly, quality produce made in continuity with old traditions, and thirdly; distinctive ways of talking and thinking about the foods that are rooted in a language and a place but open to the world. In other words we have here something that might rightly be called a food culture. An ensemble of foods, methods, uses and names that was passed on and developed from generation to generation, enriched by outside influences and ever-changing, but retaining its own identity. A culture – a collective human creation – to do with food – which is what people eat. And very specifically, a Welsh food culture, made of this land and by its people, almost disappeared but now rediscovering itself.

The future

That might be an appropriate point at which to end a book on the story of Welsh food – except that to end a tale with one's gaze firmly fixed on a past full of near-misses and heroic failures would simply be too stereotypically Welsh. In my opinion, when we consider the horizon ahead, the current rediscovery of Welsh food, and the importance of redeveloping a mixed food economy here that does not depend so entirely on outside imports and just-in-time supermarket chains, seems just in the nick of time. Global climate destabilization is accelerating, and is driving political instability, food insecurity and mass movements of people, and slowly but surely making more and more of the world uninhabitable and unfarmable. At the same time, the rapid adoption of digital technologies into every part of Western life has created social, economic and political ruptures that have already impacted the world of food, and will continue to do so. Food itself has become more politicized and polarized than perhaps ever before, with debates about veganism, rewilding, subsidies and the future of farming redounding round the echo chambers of the internet and the airwaves.

Against this backdrop, the re-growth of a local food economy, rooted in a local food culture in a place like Wales, feels like exactly the kind of asynchronous response that is needed. By asynchronous, I mean a response that operates on an entirely different level, and according to entirely different rules and logic, to the forces that threaten us. As Einstein famously put it, 'we cannot solve our problems with the same thinking we used when we created them'. So does it matter to us that people rather than machines make the food we eat? Does it matter that everyone has access to good, healthy food they can afford? Does it matter to us that this land – and others like it – is one populated by farmers? If it does, and we see those things as good in and of themselves, then we have a basis for discussion about a future that necessarily includes rural employment; necessarily upholds centuries of tradition; necessarily creates the space for human connection between the producer and the consumer (*consumo* is Latin for 'I eat'), and much more. We can then, once we have this baseline for discussion, insist that farmers and producers do what so many are already doing, as we have seen in this book – namely farm in a way that increases, rather than decreases biodiversity. We can, and doubtless should, as a society eat less meat – but better meat, thus only returning to what was de facto the case for most of our ancestors throughout the long ages of the world. There are templates for this in so much of the Welsh food history we have been exploring. There is nothing desirable about returning to the past, if that were even possible; but much to be gained from re-evaluating our own norms by considering them in the light of the past.

A good example of this lies in the fact that traditional Welsh food – like all great cuisines – is the product of a mixed food and farming economy. The fact that many of the foods and foodstuffs in this book have not all continued to be produced in Wales is, in many cases, due to the disappearance of mixed farming in the country over the latter half of the 20th century. As Rhys Lougher, Anne Parry, Carwyn Adams and Alex Simmens all explained through the lenses of the food they produce, the drive towards specialization has completely reshaped Welsh farming over the decades since the Second World War, and has, on the whole, led to a marked reduction in the variety of food produced on Welsh farms. The current state of affairs, with an almost exclusive emphasis on live-stock rearing, is, however, not sustainable, neither economically nor ecologically. There is a dawning realization in both the food and farming sectors that monocultures are not the way to go for human or planetary health, and a convincing case has been made that a mixed economy of small farms could not only lead to better food, but also greater rural employment.[4] For Welsh food, this is the *sine qua non* of not only rediscovering and developing old food trad-itions, but also of securing the fragile rural economy. This is also the only realistic way in which the potential of this half-dormant cuisine can be realized; an entire food economy from field to plate needs coaxing into existence once again.

The broad ingredient list of the Welsh culinary traditions also reminds us of the food production potential of all the habitats of the land and seas of a place like Wales. We know that this corner of Europe is very likely to be spared most of the worst effects of climate change, so that feeding people both here and elsewhere from this land is likely to become a moral imperative over coming decades. Studying food history is the best possible place to start for a full and nuanced understanding of what the land can produce, and nowhere is this more true than those parts of the world where the modern industrial economy and food system have swallowed and distorted native traditions. Apple-growing in Wales is a good case in point, though the principle could be applied to countless societies the world over. The UK as a whole currently only produces 20% of the apples eaten in the country, and Wales close to zero.[5] We now know that traditionally managed orchards are one of the single most biodiverse ecosystems that can exist in northern Europe, and they can also produce significant crops of fruit, honey, dairy and meat (from sheep) and wood from the same land. So for the sake of rural employment, the future of our birds and insects and the survival of native traditions, it seems obvious that those Welsh river valleys that a century ago teemed with orchards need refilling with new ones. This flies in the face of the economic wisdom that saw 95–98% of Welsh orchards grubbed up in the twentieth century; but then again, that economic logic has also come close to destroying the basis of life itself.

Other examples abound, and, again, what is true for Wales will be true, in different ways, for so many nations and regions around the world. Vegetable production should be scaled up significantly, as should grain growing; and then the economic superstructure of mills and millers, market gardeners and bakers can grow up around them. And none of this is a zero-sum game: the losers from a Blaencamel in every town, and *Hen Gymro* in every valley are not the Loughers, the Pritchards or *Caws Cenarth*; they are multi-national corporations, and supermarkets with no stake in Welsh futures.

And there are also ecological lessons to be gained from studying the carrying capacity of this land and shore, as we saw in the contrasting tales of oysters and cockles. Government policy makes a significant difference to whether the potential of the land is used, as the tale of Welsh sea salt production makes clear. We are now in a position, unlike most of our ancestors, where we can research, experiment and innovate to find the best ways to produce more food from the land and seas of places like Wales, whilst also locking in carbon and increasing biodiversity. Is there a task more urgent than this for the wellbeing of both current and future generations? If we doubled down to this work in earnest, could we even see a food and farming renaissance in Wales that formed the basis for a good life for all the future inhabitants of this land, whatever their origins?

All this could be done in the modern, internet-powered vacuum of possibilities without so much as a glance to the past. We could, for instance, decide to keep our shelves stocked with *bara brith*, but finally acknowledge that the age of buttermilk and salty butter has now gone and the day of yoghurt and margarine has long since come. There is much to be grateful for in the open door we currently have to ingredients, dishes, production methods adopted and adapted from anywhere in the world. But most of the best dishes are time-worn; most of the best food knows where it came from, what story it fits into and even what story it is a reaction against.

And so to base the food economy of the future on the foods of a faceless global village and a soulless global market would be to do not just Wales but the entire world a disservice.

The re-establishment in public discourse of a Welsh food culture, with its long history, its ingredients and methods, provides the possibility of a rooted baseline for the future of food in this country; open to change, but aware of its provenance. There is comfort, there can be a very rightful pride in knowing that this loaf was made from this heritage flour, grown ten miles away on Ceredigion soil and milled in the village named after the local river's many mills. Or in eating a cawl in 2050, made with mutton that grazed on *ffridd*-land rich in insect life from a flock hefted to it for hundreds of years. Or in cider made from native varieties grown in an orchard of mature, standard apple trees planted in 2020 on some of those same Monmouthshire fields that had long been under orchard but were grubbed up in the 1960s. That kind of pleasure, and pride, is not the kind that led to the interlocking crises I mentioned earlier. It might well, then, offer itself as the basis of a very different, but deeply rooted, kind of future.

RECOMMENDED SUPPLIERS

I hope that after reading this book you will be inspired to find out who your local baker, dairy, veg grower, apiarist or vintner is and support their business – as well as those mentioned in this book. Here are the contact details and addresses of the suppliers featured in the book – as well as one or two others that make a particular point of sourcing and promoting excellent Welsh foods:

Felin Ganol
Llanrhystud
Ceredigion SY23 5AL
felinganol.co.uk

Andy's Bread
Llanidloes
Unit 6a, Parc Derwen Fawr
Llanidloes SY18 6FE
andysbread.co.uk

Caws Cenarth
Fferm Glyneithinog
Lancych
Boncath SA37 0LH
cawscenarth.co.uk

Caws Hafod Cheese
Bwlchwernen Fawr
Lampeter SA48 8PS
hafodcheese.co.uk

The Welsh Cheese Company
welshcheesecompany.co.uk

Selwyn's
selwynsseafoods.com

Gower Salt Marsh Lamb
Weobley Castle
Llanrhidian
Swansea SA3 1HB

Halen Môn
Tŷ Halen
Brynsiencyn
Ynys Môn LL61 6TQ

Tŷ Tanglwyst dairy
tytanglwystdairy.com

Llanblethian orchards
Crossways
Cowbridge CF71 7LJ
llancider.wales

Ferry Cabin
Ferryside SA17 5SF

Blaencamel Farm
Cilcennin
Lampeter
Ceredigion
SA48 8BB
facebook.com/blaencamelfarm

Eateries

Wright's Food Emporium
Golden Grove Arms
Llanarthne
Carmarthen
SA32 8JU

Bara Menyn
45 Heol Santes Fair
Aberteifi / Cardigan
SA43 1HA
baramenynbakehouse.co.uk

DIOLCHIADAU /
ACKNOWLEDGEMENTS

This book, four years in the making, has been a true pleasure to write but a greater pleasure still to research. That is due in great part to the wonderful farmers, growers, producers, bakers, millers and fishermen I had the privilege of meeting and getting to know, and whose stories form the living backbone to this volume. My warm thanks to all of you: for allowing me into your houses, farms and land, for illuminating and enjoyable conversations and for many a kind gift and undeserved meal. Anne and Andrew, Carwyn, Brian, Will, Rhys and John, Eluned, Andy, Alex, Paul and Jean, Peter and Anne: *Diolch o galon*. Warm thanks also to Simon and Maryann at Wright's for embodying what hospitality should be, and for much generous advice. I hope that your stories – and the stories of the countless others in Wales working to feed people well – not only continue to grow but flourish in a new way as people come to value good, local food once more.

My warm thanks go to my editor, Clare: for her support, insights and comments that have helped this book become a much richer tale than it would have been otherwise. Thank you for making this book what it is! To Natalie, Amy, Maria, Steve and the entire team at the press, for the vision to launch this imprint, the graft to pull it off, and the faith to run with this volume as one of its first titles and to Ruth for her marketing prowess. I hope the result does you all justice. *I Myrddin ap Dafydd a Mererid Hopwood – diolch am eich anogaeth a'ch geiriau caredig wrth i mi gychwyn ar daith y llyfr hwn. Diolch hefyd i Sioned ac i Mam am sylwadau craff ac anogaeth ar sawl tro. I Beti Jones hefyd, am ganiatâd i ddefnyddio cerdd hyfryd Bobi.* To Jan and Anna Bishop for kind and helpful comments on early drafts of the manuscript. And a greater debt of gratitude still to my dear and beloved wife, Sarah, who has not only read and re-read this book and given her usual incisive comments but has borne the brunt of parental responsibility too many times when I have been ensconced in a quiet study, writing away. Without your strength and stamina but above all love and encouragement, the book wouldn't have seen the light of day.

I want to end by paying tribute to the many people who paved the way before me in writing the story of Welsh food and farming, and who in chronicling vanishing ways of life have left the way open for future generations to rediscover much that is good and of value. I am indebted to all their work and can only hope that despite numerous errors and misreadings of history that doubtless remain here, and are my fault alone, enough of a true picture has been painted to be useful to others. The practice of honouring those who are now gone seems important to me, not least as there is some connection between that practice and the essential but maligned virtue of honouring those who have not yet been born; so I also hope that this collection of historical stories honours the men and above all, the women, to whom the long tale of Welsh food most of all belongs.

SELECT BIBLIOGRAPHY

There are a large number of recipe books and similar books on Welsh food aimed at the tourist market. Most of these appear to be derivative in their research, and draw their recipes from a gentle mixture of the sources below and a healthy sprinkling of human imagination. They are thus not included in this bibliography.

Welsh food history – general
Bobby Freeman, *First Catch your Peacock* (Talybont: Y Lolfa, 1980)

R. Elwyn Hughes, *Dysgl Bren a Dysgl Arian: Nodiadau ar hanes bwyd yng Nghymru* (Talybont: Y Lolfa, 2003)

S. Minwel Tibbott, *Welsh Fare* (Cowbridge: National Museum of Wales, 1976)

S. Minwel Tibbott, *Domestic Life in Wales* (Cardiff: University of Wales Press, 2002)

S. Minwel Tibbott, *Geirfa'r Gegin* (Llandysul: National Museum of Wales, 1983)

Specific foods
Bread

Bobby Freeman, *A Book of Welsh Bakestone Cookery* (Talybont: Y Lolfa, 2007)

S. Minwel Tibbott, *Baking in Wales* (Cardiff: National Museum of Wales, 1991)

Cheese

Thelma Adams, *Gwlad o Gaws a Llaeth* (Llandysul: Gomer, 2012)

Juliet Harbutt (ed.), *World Cheese Book* (London: Dorling Kindersley, 2009)

Steven Lamb, *Cheese and Dairy* (London: Bloomsbury, 2009)

Ned Palmer, *A Cheesemonger's History of the British Isles* (London: Profile, 2019)

Eurwen Richards, *Caws Cymru* (Llanrwst: Gwasg Carreg Gwalch, 2006)

Lamb, mutton and beef

Colyer, R., 'Welsh Cattle Drovers in the Nineteenth Century', *National Library of Wales Journal*, 17/4, Winter 1972

Twm Elias, *Welsh Farm Animals: Cattle* (Llanrwst: Gwasg Carreg Gwalch, 2000)

Twm Elias, *Y Porthmyn Cymreig* (Llanrwst: Gwasg Carreg Gwalch, 1987)

Salt

Hancock, S., 'An Eighteenth-Century Salt Refinery at Neyland', *Journal of the Pembrokeshire Historical Society*, 2016 *http://www.pembrokeshirehistoricalsociety.co.uk/eighteenth-century-salt-refinery-neyland/*

Hathaway, S., *Making the invisible, visible. Iron Age and Roman salt-production in Southern Britain* (unpublished thesis, Bournemouth University, 2013)

Lewis, W. J., 'Welsh Salt-Making Venture of the Sixteenth Century', *National Library of Wales Journal*, 8/4, Winter 1954

Cider

Carwyn Graves, *Apples of Wales* (Llanrwst: Gwasg Carreg Gwalch, 2018)

John Williams-Davies, *Cider Making in Wales* (Cardiff: National Museum of Wales, 1984)

Shellfish

J. Geraint Jenkins, *The Inshore Fishermen of Wales* (Stroud: Amberley Press, 2009)

Leeks

Gwyn Griffiths, *Sioni Winwns* (Llanrwst: Carreg Gwalch, 2002)

Storl and Pfyl, *Bekannte und Vergessene Gemuese* (Munich: Piper, 2013)

Other

Lyn Ebenezer, *The Thirsty Dragon* (Llanrwst: Carreg Gwalch, 2006)

Mason and Brown, *From Bath Chaps to Bara Brith* (London: Harper Press, 1999)

Traditional agriculture in Wales

Comeau and Seaman (eds), *Living off the Land: Agriculture in Wales c. 400–1600 AD* (Oxford: Oxbow books, 2019)

David Jenkins, *The Agricultural Community in Wales at the Turn of the Twentieth Century* (Cardiff: University of Wales Press, 1971)

David Jenkins, *Ar Lafar Ar Goedd* (Cymdeithas Lyfrau: Ceredigion, 2007)

J. Geraint Jenkins, *Life and Traditions in Rural Wales* (Cardiff: University of Wales Press, 2009)

George Lewis, *Haber Nant Llan Nerch Freit* (Almeley: Logaston Press, 1998)

William Linnard, *Welsh Woods and Forests* (Llandysul: Gomer, 2000)

Catherine Owen, Lloyd Jones, Eurwyn Wiliam, *Bronhaul: Y Tyddyn ar y mynydd* (Llanrwst: Carreg Gwalch, 2011)

Ffransis Payne, *Cwysau* (Llandysul: Gomer, 1980)

Emlyn Richards, *Ffarmwrs Môn* (Talybont: Y Lolfa, 2013)

Margaret Roberts, *Oes o Fyw ar y Mynydd* (Caernarfon: Gwasg Gwynedd, 1979)

Colin Thomas, 'Thirteenth century Farm Economies in North Wales', *Agricultural History Review*, 16/1 (1968)

Anne Williams, *Meddyginiaethu Gwerin Cymru* (Talybont: Y Lolfa, 2017)

Contemporary accounts of Welsh life and food

Rachel Bromwich (ed.), *Trioedd Ynys Prydein: The Triads of the Island of Britain* (Cardiff: University of Wales Press, 2014)

Walter Davies, *Agricultural Survey of North Wales* (London: 1810)

Walter Davies, *Agricultural Survey of South Wales* (London: 1815)

Daniel Defoe, *'A Tour Thro' the Whole Island of Great Britain, Divided into Circuits or Journies'* (1727)

Edward Donovan, *Descriptive Excursions through South Wales and Monmouthshire, in the Year 1804 and the Four Preceding Summers* (London: 1805)

David Lloyd Owen, *A Wilder Wales* (Cardigan: Parthian, 2017)

Marie Trevelyan, *Glimpses of Welsh Life and Character* (1893)
https://sublimewales.wordpress.com/

Welsh economic and social history

John Davies, *The History of Wales* (London: Penguin, 1990)

Russell Davies, *Hope and Heartbreak: A Social History of Wales and the Welsh, 1776–1871* (Cardiff: University of Wales Press, 2005)

Edwards, Lane and Redknap, *Early Medieval Wales: An updated framework for archaeological research* (2010)

Helen Fulton (ed.), *Urban Culture in Medieval Wales* (Cardiff: University of Wales Press, 2012)

Trefor Owen, *The Customs and Traditions of Wales* (Cardiff: University of Wales Press, 1991)

Powell, N., 'Do Numbers Count? Towns in Early Modern Wales', *Urban History*, 32/1, 2005

Peter Smith, *Houses of the Welsh Countryside* (HMSO: 1975)

Richard Suggett, *Discovering the Historic Houses of Snowdonia*, (RCAHMW: 2014)

Richard Suggett and Greg Stevenson, *Cyflwyno Cartrefi Cefn Gwlad Cymru* (Talybont: Y Lolfa, 2010)

Thirsk, Barley and Willmore (eds), *The Agrarian History of England and Wales: Volume 5, The Buildings of the Countryside, 1500–1750* (Cambridge: Cambridge University Press, 1967)

Steven Thompson, *Unemployment, Poverty and Health in Interwar South Wales* (Cardiff: University of Wales Press, 2006)

Elizabeth Whittle, *The Historic Gardens of Wales* (London: HMSO, 1992)

Eurwyn Wiliam, *Y Bwthyn Cymreig* (Aberystwyth: CBHC, 2010)

Glanmor Williams, *Recovery, Reorientation and Reformation: Wales 1415–1642* (Oxford: Oxford University Press, 1987)

Welsh ecology and natural history

William Condry, *The Natural History of Wales* (London: Bloomsbury, 1981)

Richard Hartnup, *Gold Under Bracken* (Talybont: Y Lolfa, 2011)

George Monbiot, *Feral* (London: Penguin, 2014)

Local History

Mike Benbough-Jackson, *Cardiganshire: The concise history* (Cardiff: University of Wales Press, 2007)

Penny David, *Rooted in History: Celebrating Carmarthenshire's parks and gardens* (Lampeter: Fern Press, 2017)

C. J. O. Evans, *Glamorgan: Its history and topography* (Cardiff: Williams Lewis, 1943)

Max Lieberman, *The March of Wales, 1067–1300* (Cardiff: University of Wales Press, 2008)

Jonathan Mullard, *Gower* (London: Collins, 2006)

Jonathan Mullard, *Pembrokeshire* (London: Collins, 2020)

Palmer, David, and Laidlaw, *Historic Parks and Gardens in Ceredigion* (Talybont: Y Lolfa, 2004)

David Pretty, *Anglesey: The concise history* (Cardiff: University of Wales Press, 2005)

J. Mansel Thomas, *Yesterday's Gower* (Llandysul: Gomer, 1982)

Food histories of neighbouring societies

Dorothy Hartley, *Food in England* (London: Macdonald, 1985)

Margaret Hickey, *Ireland's Green Larder* (London: Unbound, 2018)

Erwin Seitz, *Die Verfeinerung der Deutschen* (Berlin: Insel Verlag, 2011)

Maryann Tebben, *Savoir-Faire: A history of food in France* (London: Reaktion,2020)

Joan Thirsk, *Alternative Agriculture* (Oxford: Oxford University Press, 1997)

Joan Thirsk, *Food in Early Modern England* (London: Continuum, 2006)

Food and the Future

Michael Pollan, *In Defence of Food* (London: Penguin, 2008)

Mark Price, *The Food Lover's Handbook* (London: Penguin, 2016)

Chris Smaje, *A Small Farm Future* (London: Chelsea Green, 2020)

NOTES

Introduction

1. Hartnup, *Gold under Bracken*, 15.
2. I will explore this topic, and the interplay between the nature and culture of Wales over the past 10,000 years in my next book, due out with UWP late 2023.
3. Gower, *The Story of Wales*, 204.
4. An appropriate term to use for Wales pre-1536, though much more problematic for the following centuries.
5. There is a need for an authoritative history of Welsh food; this is not that book, but it can hopefully make a meaningful contribution to the need, not least in bringing together many of the key sources and starting points for further work.
6. Jenkins, *Life and Tradition in Rural Wales*; cf. Hughes, *Dysgl Bren a dysgl arian*.
7. Youngs, 'The Townswomen of Wales', in Fulton (ed.), *Urban Culture in Medieval Wales*, 166.
8. Smith, *Medical Officer's Report to the Committee of the Privy Council. Sixth Report (1863)*, Appendix VI and VII, Food of the Lowest Classes, British Parliamentary Papers, 1864.
9. Williams, *Recovery, Reorientation and Reformation*, 427.
10. Pretty, *Anglesey: The Concise History*, 42.
11. Powell, 'Do Numbers Count?', 67.
12. Powell, 'Do Numbers Count?', 59.
13. Graves, *Apples of Wales*, 36.
14. Williams, *Recovery, Reorientation and Reformation*, 113.
15. Miller, 'A Dangerous Revolutionary Force Amongst Us', 419–38.
16. Hughes, *Dysgl bren a dysgl arian*, 200–21.

17. https://sublimewales.wordpress.com/material-culture/occupations/agriculture/agricultural-reports/

18. Thomas, *Yesterday's Gower*, 32.

Chapter 1

1. Edwards, Lane and Redknap, *Early Medieval Wales*, 5.

2. Hughes, *Dysgl bren a dysgl arian*, 18.

3. Hughes, *Dysgl bren a dysgl arian*, 104.

4. Tibbott, *Baking in Wales*, 9.

5. Freeman, *First Catch your Peacock*, 90.

6. Tibbott, *Baking in Wales*, 19–23.

7. Owen, *A Wilder Wales*, 132.

8. Thirsk et al. (eds), *The Agrarian History of England and Wales: Volume 5*, 18.

9. Price, *The Food Lover's handbook*, 137.

10. www.welshgrainforum.co.uk/hen-gymro

11. www.barasadwrn.wordpress.com/2018/10/07/hen-gymro/amp

12. http://www.wheat-gateway.org.uk/hub.php?ID=41

13. Pollan, *In Defence of Food*, 121.

14. For reasons internal to the National Trust. But it was grown at Green Acres Farm in Shifnal and in Builth by Graham Morris in the 2020 season, so the story continues …

Chapter 2

1. Tibbott, *Domestic Life in Wales*, 68.

2. *South Wales Echo*, 31 July 1896.

3. Richards, *Caws Cymru*, 14.

4. Tibbott, *Domestic Life in Wales*, 72.

5. Tibbott, *Domestic Life in Wales*, 72.

6. Palmer, *Cheesemonger's History of Britain*, 18.

7. Cf. Roberts, *Oes o fyw ar y mynydd*.

8. Owen, *A Wilder Wales*, 32.

9. Freeman, *First Catch your Peacock*, 31.

10. Thirsk, *Food in Early Modern England*, 279.

11. Richards, *Caws Cymru*, 12.

12. Owen, *A Wilder Wales*, 257.

13. Richards, *Caws Cymru*, 9.

14. Hartley, *Food in England*, 486.
15. Richards, *Caws Cymru*, 12.
16. Richards, *Caws Cymru*, 82.
17. https://en.wikipedia.org/wiki/Cheddar_cheese
18. Tibbott, *Domestic Life in Wales*, 70.
19. Richards, *Caws Cymru*, 28.
20. Richards, *Caws Cymru*, 28.
21. Tibbott, *Domestic Life in Wales*, 60.
22. Owen, *A Wilder Wales*, 321.
23. Tibbott, *Domestic Life in Wales*, 70.
24. Richards, *Caws Cymru*, 15.
25. Richards, *Caws Cymru*, 53.
26. Harbutt (ed.), *World Cheese Book*, 216.
27. Adams, *Gwlad o gaws a llaeth*, 83.
28. Cf. https://www.sciencedirect.com/science/article/abs/pii/S0958694616303259

Chapter 3

1. Known to vary in colour across this spectrum: www.britannica.com/science/laver
2. Umami – a category of taste in food (besides sweet, sour, salt and bitter), corresponding very roughly to what is commonly called 'savoury'.
3. https://en.wikipedia.org/wiki/Porphyra
4. Mullard, *Pembrokeshire*, 182.
5. https://www.beachfood.co.uk/blog/The+Story+of+Laver+Seaweed+in+Wales
6. https://www.beachfood.co.uk/blog/LAVER+SEAWEED+ONE+of+the+FOOD+WONDERS+OF+THE+WORLD
7. Tibbott, *Welsh Fare*, 66.
8. Thompson, *Unemployment, Poverty and Health in Interwar South Wales*, 87.
9. Freeman, *First Catch your Peacock*, 170.
10. http://www.laverbread.com/laverbread-recipes/#lquiche
11. https://www.countryfile.com/countryfile-tv-show/helen-skelton-silage-seaweed-and-sup/
12. https://en.wikipedia.org/wiki/Laverbread

13. http://www.gallowaywildfoods.com/laver-seaweed-edibility-identification-distribution/

14. Mullard, *Gower*, 69.

15. Donovan, *Descriptive Excursions through South Wales and Monmouthshire*, 360.

16. https://sublimewales.wordpress.com/material-culture/occupations/agriculture/agricultural-reports/

17. https://sublimewales.wordpress.com/material-culture/occupations/agriculture/agricultural-reports/

18. Thirsk, *Food in Early Modern England*, 146.

19. Donovan, *Descriptive Excursions through South Wales and Monmouthshire, in the year 1804 and the four preceding summers*, 360.

20. Fenton, Richard, 1807, from https://sublimewales.wordpress.com/material-culture/occupations/agriculture/agricultural-reports/

21. Davies, *Agricultural Survey of South Wales*.

22. *Circeii for oysters, sea-urchins come from Misenum,*
    Tarentum, the home of luxury, boasts wide scallops.
    No one can idly claim skill in the culinary arts,
    Not without mastering first the subtle science of flavours.
    Horace, Satires, Book 2, Satire 4.

23. Mullard, *Gower*, 144.

24. Lewis Morris (1748), cited in https://sublimewales.wordpress.com/material-culture/occupations/agriculture/agricultural-reports/

25. Richard Llwyd (1832), cited in https://sublimewales.wordpress.com/material-culture/occupations/agriculture/agricultural-reports/

26. Lewis Morris (1748), cited in https://sublimewales.wordpress.com/material-culture/occupations/agriculture/agricultural-reports/

27. Thomas John (1775), cited in https://sublimewales.wordpress.com/material-culture/occupations/agriculture/agricultural-reports/

28. George Owen (1603), cited in https://sublimewales.wordpress.com/material-culture/occupations/agriculture/agricultural-reports/

29. Richard Fenton (1804), cited in https://sublimewales.wordpress.com/material-culture/occupations/agriculture/agricultural-reports/

30. Mullard, *Gower*, 145.

31. Mullard, *Gower*, 144.

32. Mullard, *Pembrokeshire*, 244.

33. cockle and mussel women | Welsh Costume / Gwisg Gymreig (wordpress .com)

34. Trevelyan, *Glimpses of Welsh Life and Character*, 165–6.

35. Mullard, *Gower*, 232.

36. Mullard, *Gower*, 234.

Chapter 4

1. Whittingstall et al. (eds), *River Cottage A–Z*, 328.

2. Protected Geographical Indication (PGI) is a status awarded by the European Commission that protects and promotes named regional food products that have a reputation or noted characteristics specific to an area.

3. Price, *The Food Lover's handbook*, 162.

4. Bromwich (ed.), *Trioedd Ynys Prydein: The Triads of the Island of Britain*, 126.

5. Thirsk, *Food in Early Modern England*, 235.

6. Elias, *Y Porthmyn Cymreig*, 7.

7. Elias, *Y Porthmyn Cymreig*, 11.

8. Elias, *Y Porthmyn Cymreig*, 18.

9. Colyer, 'Welsh Cattle Drovers in the Nineteenth Century'.

10. Colyer, 'Welsh Cattle Drovers in the Nineteenth Century'.

11. Elias, *Y Porthmyn Cymreig*, 8.

12. Elias, *Y Porthmyn Cymreig*, 41.

13. Elias, *Y Porthmyn Cymreig*, 8.

14. Davies, *Hope and Heartbreak*, 45.

15. Owen, *A Wilder Wales*, 98.

16. Hartley, *Food in England*, 139.

17. https://www.bbc.co.uk/news/uk-wales-48503111

18. https://www.nationaltrust.org.uk/whiteford-and-north-gower/features/cwm-ivy-where-the-sea-comes-in

Chapter 5

1. https://bmjopen.bmj.com/content/4/4/e004549

2. Prior, *Farmers in Prehistoric Britain*, 215

3. Hathaway, S., *Making the invisible, visible*.

4. A copy can be found in the *Oxford Book of Welsh Verse* (1962), p. 72, and in English translation in Clancy, *Medieval Welsh Lyrics* (1965), p. 110.

5. https://biography.wales/article/s-MADO-BEN-1320

6. Hughes, *Dysgl bren a Dysgl Arian*, 22.

7. https://en.wikipedia.org/wiki/Salt_in_Cheshire

8. https://www.saltassociation.co.uk/education/salt-history/roman-times/lead-salt-pans/

9. Gower, *Mullard*, 85–6.

10. http://www.thisisgower.co.uk/discover/historical-features/salthouse/

11. Lewis, 'Welsh Salt-Making Venture of the Sixteenth Century'.

12. Hughes, *Dysgl bren a dysgl arian*, 18.

13. Owen, *A Wilder Wales*, 167.

14. Owen, *A Wilder Wales*, 257.

15. Hartley, *Food in England*, 103.

16. Freeman, *First Catch your Peacock*, 118.

17. Thirsk, *Food in Early Modern England*, 170.

18. Tibbott, *Welsh Fare*, 18.

19. Mullard, *Gower*, 85.

20. Hancock, 'An Eighteenth-Century Salt Refinery at Neyland'.

Chapter 6

1. Suggett, *Discovering the historic houses of Snowdonia*, 85 and 111.

2. Lamb, *River Cottage: Cheese and Dairy*, 18.

3. Freeman, *First Catch your Peacock*, 228.

4. Tibbott, *Welsh Fare*, 53.

5. Tibbott, *Welsh Fare*, 53.

6. Tibbott, *Baking in Wales*, 9.

7. Tibbott, *Baking in Wales*, 11.

8. Tibbott, *Welsh fare*, 28–9.

9. Tibbott, *Welsh fare*, 13.

Chapter 7

1. Williams-Davies, *Cider Making in Wales*, 2.

2. Graves, *Apples of Wales*, 70.

3. Graves, *Apples of Wales*, 25.

4. Porter, *Welsh Marches Pomona*, 10.

5. Williams-Davies, *Cider Making in Wales*, 16.

6. Brown, *The Apple Orchard*, 265.

7. Williams-Davies, *Cider Making in Wales*, 36.
8. Hughes, *Dysgl bren a dysgl arian*, 200–5.
9. Owen, *The Customs and Traditions of Wales*, 26.
10. Owen, *A Wilder Wales*, 166.
11. Tibbott, *Welsh Fare*, 18.

Chapter 8

1. Hughes, *Dysgl bren a dysgl arian*, 121.
2. *Tato* and *tatws* are different dialect forms for 'potato'.
3. Geiriadur Prifysgol Cymru
4. Tibbott, *Welsh Fare*, 18.
5. Freeman, *First Catch your Peacock*, 158.
6. Freeman, *First Catch your Peacock*, 21.
7. http://www.fruitnet.com/fpj/article/174161/aldis-potato-sales-rocket-in-wales
8. Kitchiner, *The Cook's Oracle: Containing Receipts for Plain Cookery*, p. 208.
9. accessed at: Potato chips and crisps | Early Tourists in Wales (wordpress.com)
10. https://gov.wales/national-diet-and-nutrition-survey-rolling-programme-ndns-results-years-2-5-combined
11. Monbiot, *Feral*, 19.
12. Benbough-Jackson, *Cardiganshire: The Concise History*, 100.
13. Freeman, *First Catch your Peacock*, 43.
14. Tibbott, *Welsh Fare*, 71.

Chapter 9

1. http://ebba.english.ucsb.edu/ballad/30222/xml accessed 17/04/21
2. *The Cambrian*, 9 March 1805.
3. *Cambrian Journal*, Alban Hevin – 1854, 190.
4. Quoted in R. Elwyn Hughes, *Dysgl Bren a Dysgl Arian*, 119.
5. Preston, Pearman and Hall, 'Archaeophytes in Britain', 257–94, https://doi.org/10.1111/j.1095-8339.2004.00284.x
6. https://www.bbc.co.uk/news/uk-wales-23754235
7. Ellis, *Welsh Tribal Law and Custom in the Middle Ages*, 38.
8. Storl and Pfyl, *Bekannte und Vergessene Gemüse*, 118–23.
9. Thirsk, *Food in Early Modern England*, 73.

10. Storl and Pfyl, *Bekannte und Vergessene Gemüse*, 117.
11. Davies, *Agricultural Survey of South Wales*, 3–4.
12. *Western Mail*, 3 June 1874.
13. Personal correspondence from David Barnes to the author.
14. Thirsk, *Alternative Agriculture*.
15. Smaje, *A Small Farm Future*.
16. Four full-time staff and three part-time or seasonal.

Postscript

1. https://carwyngraves.com/sbeis/
2. Calque – a word for word translation from another language.
3. https://www.architectsjournal.co.uk/archive/a-history-of-mosques-in-britain
4. See, for instance, Smaje, *A Small Farm Future*.
5. Macdonald and Gates, *Orchard: A year in England's Eden*, 195.